KV-648-760

Parents and their Children's Schools

Martin Hughes
Felicity Wikeley
Tricia Nash

BLACKWELL
Oxford UK & Cambridge USA

Copyright © Martin Hughes, Felicity Wikeley and Tricia Nash 1994

The right of Martin Hughes, Felicity Wikeley and Tricia Nash to be identified as
authors of this work has been asserted in accordance with the Copyright, Designs and
Patents Act 1988.

First published 1994

Blackwell Publishers
108 Cowley Road
Oxford OX4 1JF
UK

238 Main Street
Cambridge, Massachusetts 02142
USA

All rights reserved. Except for the quotation of short passages for the purposes of
criticism and review, no part of this publication may be reproduced, stored in a
retrieval system, or transmitted, in any form or by any means, electronic, mechanical,
photocopying, recording or otherwise, without the prior permission of the publisher.

Except in the United States of America, this book is sold subject to the condition that
it shall not, by way of trade or otherwise, be lent, resold, hired out, or otherwise
circulated without the publisher's prior consent in any form of binding or cover other
than that in which it is published and without a similar condition including this
condition being imposed on the subsequent purchaser.

British Library Cataloguing in Publication Data
A CIP catalogue record for this book is available from the British Library.

Library of Congress Cataloging-in-Publication Data
Hughes, Martin.
    Parents and their children's schools / Martin Hughes, Felicity Wikeley,
Tricia Nash.
        p.   cm.
    Includes bibliographical references (p.) and index.
    ISBN 0–631–18661–1. — ISBN 0–631–18662–X (pbk.)
    1. Home and school—Great Britain.   2. Education—Great Britain—
Parent participation.   3. Educational change—Great Britain.
I. Wikeley, Felicity.   II. Nash, Tricia.   III. Title.
LC225.33.G7H84   1994
370.19′3—dc20   93–39082
                                                                          CIP

Typeset in 11 on 13 pt Bembo
by Graphicraft Typesetters Ltd, Hong Kong
Printed in Great Britain by T.J. Press Ltd, Padstow, Cornwall

This book is printed on acid-free paper

Contents

Foreword   vii

1   A New Role for Parents   1

2   How Headteachers See Parents   20

3   Interviewing Parents   41

4   Parents as Consumers   56

5   Parents' Choice of School   78

6   Parents' Satisfaction with Schools   97

7   Parents and the National Curriculum   124

8   Parents' Knowledge about School   148

9   Parents and Assessment   172

10 Giving Parents a Voice   203

References   220

Index   224

Foreword

Mrs A is a single parent in her early twenties. She lives with her three young children in two rooms at the top of a multi-occupied house in a large city. The three children sleep in one room while everything else takes place in the other. The two eldest children attend a primary school nearby, which Mrs A chose because a friend's children already went there. She has virtually no contact with the school, apart from when her children are in trouble, and thinks the teachers see her as someone who 'doesn't want to know'. Nevertheless, Mrs A regards it as very important that her children learn all they can while they are at school, and she spends an hour each night helping her two eldest children with their reading.

Mrs B lives in a sought-after residential area in a large seaside town which still retains the 11-plus. She works part-time in her husband's business. Her three children attend a popular local primary school which she chose, she says half-jokingly, because 'there wasn't a large council estate next door'. Mrs B regularly helps her children with schoolwork at home, but feels that the school should be less dependent on her help in this way: she also feels the teachers could push the children harder than they do. Mrs B is loyal to the school and would not move her children anywhere else: however, she makes it very clear to the head and other teachers when she is not happy about something, particularly if it concerns her children's progress. She thinks the school sees her as an 'interfering old bat'.

Mrs C is working alongside her husband to establish themselves on a farm which is situated in a small picturesque village. Although they were privately educated themselves, they chose to send their children to the village primary school because they liked its small, family atmosphere and its close links with the local community. Mrs C regards her role in her children's education as very important, and is involved in a wide range of activities at the school, from fund-raising to running recorder classes. She talks to the teachers every day, and feels she is well informed about what is happening in the school. As she says: 'We know what we're getting with our school – it's right before our eyes'.

These three parents are bringing up their children in very different circumstances. They also have very different relationships with their children's schools – Mrs C is closely involved with school activities, Mrs B comes in frequently to complain, while Mrs A has no relationship at all. But despite these obvious differences, the three parents have a number of important features in common.

First, these parents all care deeply about their children's education. It is a matter of considerable importance to them that their children are happy at school, and that they gain as much as possible from their formal education. Each of these parents is prepared to invest time and energy in supporting their children's education in whatever way they feel is appropriate – whether by helping with schoolwork at home, by involving themselves in activities at school, or by making their dissatisfactions felt. As we shall see, they are not alone in this respect: this intense concern with their children's education is something they share with virtually all other parents.

A second feature which these parents have in common is that their children's schools are currently in the throes of a radical and far-reaching programme of reform. The last few years have seen the introduction of the National Curriculum, standardized assessment for all children, increased parental choice and a new system for funding schools. Each of these parents has been directly affected by the reforms, in that one of their children was among the first cohort to experience the National Curriculum during

Key Stage One (5–7 years) and to receive standardized assessment at the age of 7 years. For these parents, the current reforms are not just an academic exercise or a chance to score political points – rather, they impinge directly on their children's lives.

The third feature common to these parents is that they are part of a much larger group of parents whose comments, experiences and opinions make up the research described in this book. In the following chapters, these parents will tell us what they feel about the National Curriculum and what they learnt from their children's assessments. They will describe how they chose their children's schools, what they are seeking from a school, and whether their children's schools have provided what they want. They will also tell us how they feel about their new role as consumers of education. As we shall see, what these parents have to say casts serious doubt on many of the assumptions underlying the current reforms.

While our conclusions may be critical of what is currently happening in education, we did not set out with this specific intention. The research described here arose directly from our longstanding interest in the role of parents in their children's education (e.g. Tizard and Hughes, 1984; Hughes, 1986, 1994; Wikeley, 1986, 1989). The overriding aim of our project was to go beyond the stereotypical assumptions which are frequently made about parents, and to find out what a particular group of parents actually thought and felt about the current reforms. We believed that while parents had been given a crucial role to play in these reforms, they had been given few opportunities to comment in public on how they felt about that role. Above all, we wanted to allow a group of parents to speak for themselves on some issues of critical importance.

The structure of the book is as follows. In chapter 1 we describe the new role which parents have been given in the current reforms – that of consumers of education – and contrast it with two other ways in which they are frequently perceived – as partners and as problems. In chapter 2 we look at how parents are perceived by a group of headteachers who are centrally involved in the implementation of the reforms. Chapter 3 describes how we carried out the interviews with parents which form the basis of the book, and how we solved the various methodological problems involved. Chapters 4–9 form the core of the book, where we present the views of the parents in our study. Each chapter focuses on an issue of central concern: we examine in turn the issues of parents as consumers (chapter 4), parental choice (chapter 5), parents' satisfaction with the school (chapter 6), parents' attitude to the National Curriculum (chapter 7), parents' knowledge about what goes on in school (chapter 8) and parents' experience of standardized assessment (chapter 9). In chapter 10 we summarize our findings and consider their implications for the future.

The book is intended for anyone who is interested in what is happening in our education system, and who wants to know how the current reforms are perceived by the parents most directly involved. We hope that our readers will include teachers, students, governors, educational managers, policy-makers, politicians, academics and parents themselves. We have therefore tried to write about our research in a way that makes it accessible to such a wide-ranging readership. We have also tried not to do this at the expense of academic rigour.

Finally, we would like to acknowledge the support of many people and institutions without whose help the book could not have been written. The list includes the Leverhulme Trust and the University of Exeter for their generous financial support; Jackie Sherman and Mary MacMullen for their help in carrying out interviews and analysing data; our colleagues and friends at the School of Education, particularly Ted Wragg, for their encouragement and support; Ann Brackenridge for painstakingly compiling the index; Heather Midgley for her careful proof-reading; and our secretary Margaret Bown for her efficient and uncomplaining assistance. We also want to thank those colleagues and friends who read an earlier draft of the book and made valuable comments: the list includes Pam Greenhough, Cathie Holden, Flora Macleod, Ruth Merttens, Christine Mitchell, Christine Mortimer, Alison Mudditt, Alan Peacock, Caroline Smith, Barbara Tizard, David Vizard and Ted Wragg. Above all, we want to thank the parents, teachers and headteachers who made the research possible.

1
A New Role for Parents

Parents are having greatness thrust upon them.
*(Duncan Graham, former Chairman of the National
Curriculum Council, 1992, p. 36)*

The education system in England and Wales is currently experiencing one of the most far-reaching and radical programmes of reform ever seen. A series of Education Acts has resulted in innovations such as the National Curriculum, the standardized assessment of all children aged 7, 11, 14 and 16 years, a new system for the funding and local management of schools, and increased opportunities for parental choice. Entirely new categories of school have been created, such as City Technology Colleges and grant-maintained schools. These developments are regularly reported in the media, together with claims and counter-claims from politicians and others about their likely effect on educational standards. Meanwhile, teachers, pupils and parents attempt to make sense of an often bewildering process of change.

Yet beneath the complexity of the current reforms is an extremely simple idea. Education is to be regarded as a commodity, and schools as rival outlets which compete with each other for parents' custom. The parents' role in this educational market place is therefore of crucial importance. As consumers of education, their role is to make considered choices between schools on the basis of publicly available information, such as a school's performance in national examinations or standardized assessments.

The idea is that schools will have to raise their standards, and make public the fact that they have done so, or parents will take their custom elsewhere. And as the funding of individual schools is directly related to the number of pupils attending, a school which starts to lose custom is in grave danger of becoming extinct.

Later in this chapter we will look more closely at the new parental role of 'consumer', and at how it has become a central part of the current reforms. We will argue that this central role has been developed without any extensive consultation with parents themselves, and that it embodies a number of assumptions about parents which have never been tested. We start, however, by contrasting the role of consumer with two very different roles which parents have been given in the past. Drawing on a distinction made by Docking (1990), we refer to these as 'parents as problems' and 'parents as partners'.

Parents as problems

There has been a long tradition within the British education system that parents – or at least, particular groups of parents – are to be seen primarily as problems. They are considered to possess certain attitudes, or bring up their children in certain ways, which make it difficult, if not impossible, for schools to do their job properly. As a consequence, teachers may come to feel that they are engaged in an uphill struggle against the adverse effects of the home environment.

Docking (1990) suggests that while parents have always been regarded as problems, the kind of problem which they are seen as presenting has changed over the years. In the last century, for example, the early Church schools saw themselves as rescuing children from parental moral decadence, while the later Board schools saw themselves as removing children from parental exploitation. In the early years of this century teachers were frequently urged to impress school values on the home, particularly in the areas of moral and physical welfare. Indeed, the influential Hadow Report on Nursery and Infant Schools (Board of Education, 1931) noted with approval the beneficial effects on health and hygiene which had resulted from teachers talking about these matters to groups of parents.

In the 1960s the main criticism levelled at parents was that many of them were not sufficiently interested in their children's education. This concern was fuelled by the publication of a number of research studies which appeared to relate parents' attitudes to their children's achievements. One of the most influential of these studies was *The Home and the School* by Douglas (1964), which found that children's academic achievement was strongly affected by factors in their home backgrounds. In particular, parental interest in education, as assessed by their children's teachers, was found to have a greater effect than other factors, such as family size.

A similar finding was reported by the Plowden Committee (Central Advisory Committee for Education, 1967), which concluded from its own research that variation in parental attitudes was one of the main factors underlying variations in children's school achievement. In order to improve matters, Plowden outlined a five-point programme for developing relationships with parents. The programme consisted of a welcome to the school, regular meetings between parents and teachers, open days for parents to see their children's work, information for parents about their child's progress and general school activities, and annual written reports. While in retrospect the Plowden programme looks relatively unambitious, at the time these recommendations constituted a major step forward in home/school relationships.

The 1970s saw the emergence of a different type of parental 'problem', namely their language. Increasing prominence was given to the idea that the relative underachievement of working-class children in school was due to linguistic problems, and that these in turn were due to inadequacies in the way the children were talked to by their parents at home. This idea, which was known as the theory of 'language deficit' or 'verbal deprivation', was often supported by reference to the highly influential work of Bernstein (1971), Tough (1976) and the Bullock Report (Department of Education and Science, 1975). Teachers were therefore urged to influence the language used in working-class homes, or at least to neutralize its effects in the classroom by providing more appropriate language models.

In the 1980s the language deficit theory was challenged by a number of research studies which looked more closely at the language actually used by parents of different social backgrounds when talking to their children at home (Tizard and Hughes, 1984; Wells, 1984, 1987). The former study, for example, concluded that the conversations which took place in working-class homes were just as frequent and extensive as those taking place in middle-class homes, and that most working-class children appeared to be growing up in a rich linguistic environment. Nevertheless, in spite of such findings, the theory of language deficit is still widely held, and the language used by working-class parents at home is often regarded as a major source of children's difficulties in school (Hughes, 1994). In the words of one reception-class teacher:

Toxic childhood

> I don't like to blame the parents – they try very hard – but we do get the children straight from home, so what else can we blame it on?

A classic statement of the view that parents are essentially problems was made in 1985 by Dame Mary Warnock, when she presented the Richard Dimbleby lecture on BBC television. Dame Warnock's educational credentials included a successful academic career at Oxford and Cambridge, six years as headteacher of Oxford High School, and chairing the Warnock Committee on special educational needs. The theme of her Dimbleby lecture was the need to increase the professional standing of teachers. At one point she turned to the subject of parents:

> Of course, a lot of the trouble lies with the parents. . . . Looking back on my days as a headmistress, I can see that we at school divided parents roughly into two categories: the pushy and the indifferent. The pushy parent is always certain that he is right, both in his estimation of his child's ability, and in his views on what should be taught at school, and by what method. . . . His guiding principle is that his child is superior to others. . . . The indifferent parent is, obviously, less trouble. His name does not produce groans when mentioned in the staffroom. . . . For the indifferent parent, school is a tiresome necessity, the teachers intruders no more welcome than tax-collectors. (p. 12)

Warnock appears to be suggesting here that all parents are problems of some kind, either because they show too much interest in their child's education or because they show too little. Warnock does not say whether any parents manage to show just the right level of interest – or indeed, what this level would be – in order to escape being categorized one way or the other.

The parents whom Warnock dealt with as headteacher at Oxford High School were probably somewhat different from those encountered by Malcolm Gooch, a teacher in an inner-city primary school. Nevertheless, both saw their parents as essentially problematic. Writing in 1990, Gooch painted a graphic description of the difficulties he was currently facing, such as unruly and anti-social behaviour, resistance to learning, lack of concentration, and little or no regard for other children. He continued:

> I believe that many of the problems are caused by poor parenting, a further result of which is that much of what the school achieves is nullified or lost at the end of each day and to a greater extent during holidays. Thus each day we start again to re-learn the lessons of yesterday. (*The Guardian*, 24 July 1990)

It is clear that the perception of parents as problems has a long history in the British education system. Such a perception does not fit easily with the current idea that parents – of whatever social class – should instead be regarded as consumers. Indeed, if parents are seen as having little interest in their children's education or little knowledge about what goes on in schools, or if they are considered to hold values which are antithetical to those of the school, then there may be substantial resistance amongst professionals to the idea that they should be allowed to make critical decisions about their children's education.

Parents as partners

An alternative and more positive perception of parents is to see them as partners in the educational process. As Docking (1990) points out, such partnerships can take one of two main forms. On the one hand, parents can be seen as partnering teachers in the day-to-day business of helping children learn, particularly through involvement in specific areas of the curriculum. On the other hand, parents can also be seen as partners in the decision-making processes of schools, particularly through involvement on the school's governing body. We will look at each aspect in turn.

The idea of involving parents directly in their children's learning has a long history. For example, the practice of sending reading books home so that parents can hear their children read has been going on in some parts of the country for most of this century. This approach received a major boost in the 1980s with the publication of research studies showing how effective it could be. Particularly influential were the Haringey Reading Project (Tizard, Schofield and Hewison, 1982), the Belfield Reading Project (Hannon and Jackson, 1987), the PACT project in Inner London (Griffiths and Hamilton, 1984) and the Community Education Development Centre (CEDC) project in Coventry (Widlake and Macleod, 1985). All these projects demonstrated the value of involving parents in children's reading, although not all of them produced statistically significant gains on reading test scores. Nevertheless, their findings stimulated and sustained the growing interest amongst teachers in developing this kind of partnership with parents. By the end of the 1980s, it had become common practice amongst primary schools to involve parents in some way in their children's reading.

From reading, it was a short step towards involving parents in other areas of the curriculum, such as mathematics. The most successful attempt to do this has undoubtedly been the IMPACT project (Merttens and Vass, 1990). The basic idea of IMPACT is simple: each week children take home a mathematical activity – either one produced by the IMPACT team or one devised by their teacher – and carry it out with their parents at home. The project started from small beginnings in 1985, involving a few schools in Inner London. By the end of the decade, it had grown into a massive operation, involving several thousand schools in over 50 local authorities around the country. Although a systematic evaluation of IMPACT in terms of its effects on children's learning has not yet been completed and published, its value is clearly attested to by the large number of teachers who have incorporated it into their classroom practice.

The other main form of partnership which emerged in the 1980s was the growing presence of parents on the governing bodies of schools. This development, which was part of a more general movement towards 'accountability' in education and other public services, was encouraged during the 1980s by a series of Education Acts. The 1980 Education Act allowed for up to two parents on the governing body of each school, while the 1986 Education Act increased the proportion of parent governors and allowed a parent to become the chair-person. The 1988 Education Reform Act extended the duties and responsibilities of governing bodies to include responsibility for ensuring that the National Curriculum was followed in each school: in addition, under the new arrangements for the local management of schools, the governing body was given major responsibility for the school's budget and for making crucial decisions about the employment and dismissal of teaching staff. The governing body was also given the power to 'opt out' of local authority control and apply for grant-maintained status, provided that enough parents were in favour.

These changes in legislation have enormously increased the potential for parents to be partners in the business of running their children's schools. Nevertheless, research has shown that such involvement is very much a minority pursuit (e.g. Golby and Lane, 1989). This is partly because only a handful of parents in any one school can ever be significantly involved in this way, but also because the demands and responsibilities placed on governors, and the skills required to perform their duties successfully, deter the vast majority of parents from becoming involved. Indeed, the shortage of parent governors had become so acute in 1992 that the Department of Education and Science was forced to launch a major recruitment campaign, in the form of leaflets and national TV advertisements.

While these developing forms of partnership have been welcomed by many parents and teachers, it is not immediately apparent how far the role of partner fits with that of consumer. Indeed, it could be argued that the two roles embody two very different relationships with schools. A partner might be seen as someone who is closely involved with a school, someone who shares – and even helps to shape – the aims of the school, and is committed to putting these aims into practice. In contrast, a consumer might be seen as someone who is on the outside, judging a school's performance from a distant vantage point. The tension between these two different parental roles is an issue which reappears throughout this book.

Parents as consumers

The idea that parents should be seen as consumers of education first emerged in the writings of various right-wing educationalists during the late 1970s and 1980s (e.g. Cox and Boyson, 1977; Hillgate Group, 1986, 1987; Flew, 1987; Sexton, 1987). These writers put forward a number of criticisms of the state education system and proposed various alternatives, many of which were subsequently incorporated into the current reforms. While they did not necessarily agree on every point, there was a great deal of consensus in what they were saying.

A common starting point was the assumption that educational standards were falling, and that this was due to the misguided pursuit of egalitarian policies, such as comprehensive education, or to progressive teaching methods:

> It must always be remembered that the deterioration in British education has arisen partly because schools have been treated as instruments for equalising, rather than instructing, children. Merit, competition and self-esteem have been devalued or repudiated; the teaching of facts has given way to the inculcation of opinion; education has often been confounded with indoctrination; and in many places there is a serious risk of disciplined study being entirely swamped by an amorphous tide of easy-going discussion and idle play. (Hillgate Group, 1987, p. 2)

Several of these writers noted that such faults were not to be found in the private sector, and that therefore the goal must be to create an 'independent education for all'. This in turn meant that schools would have to be freed from state control, and especially from local authority control, and a genuine market in education created. As Sexton (1987) put it:

The only choice left is to devolve the system to the schools themselves, and to create a direct relationship between the suppliers of
education, the schools and the teachers, and the consumers, the
parents and their children. It is to create, as near as practicable, a
'free market' in education. To use a popular word, it is in some
sense to 'privatise' the State education system. (p. 10)

The likely effects of such a policy on schools were made starkly
clear by the Hillgate Group (1986):

Their survival should depend on their ability to satisfy their customers. And their principal customers are parents, who should
therefore be free to place their custom where they wish, in order
that educational institutions should be shaped, controlled and
nourished by their demand. . . . Schools will have to work to stay
in business, and the worse their results, the more likely they will
be to go to the wall. (pp. 7, 16)

These ideas exerted a major influence on the 1988 Education
Reform Act, the prime legislative instrument of the current
reforms. The main purpose of the Act was to introduce the
National Curriculum and standardized assessment, to remove some
of the obstacles to parental choice and to establish a new system
for the local management of schools. However, the written legislation contains little insight into the kind of thinking on which
it is based. For this, we have to look at what was actually said in
the House of Commons at the time. The following comments,
for example, were made by the then Secretary of State for Education, Kenneth Baker, when he introduced the Bill at the end of
1987. Baker started by criticizing the state education system on
the grounds that:

It has become producer-dominated. It has not proved sensitive to
the demands for change that have become ever more urgent over
the past 10 years. This Bill will create a new framework, which
will raise standards, extend choice, and produce a better educated
Britain. . . . If we are to implement the principle of the 1944 Education Act that children should be 'educated in accordance with the
wishes of their parents', then we must give consumers of education a central part in decision making. That means freeing schools

and colleges to deliver the standards that parents and employers want. It means encouraging the consumer to expect and demand that all educational bodies do the best job possible. In a word it means choice. . . . For the first time in 80 years they [local education authorities] will face competition in the provision of free education, so standards will rise in all schools as we introduce a competitive spirit into the provision of education – and at no extra cost to the consumer. (*Hansard*, 1 December 1987)

This important passage contains many echoes of the earlier arguments put forward by Sexton and the Hillgate Group. Baker introduces here the central notion of parents as 'consumers of education', and contrasts this with the 'producers', whom he claims have been dominating the system to its detriment for too long. Baker does not spell out here who these 'producers' are, but it must be assumed that they are teachers, local authorities and other educational 'experts' such as advisers and Her Majesty's Inspectorate. He goes on to suggest that this producer domination has resulted in low educational standards; indeed, the implication could be drawn that these producers of education – unlike parents and employers – do not actually want high educational standards. The solution to the problem is clear. Schools and colleges must be 'freed' to 'deliver the standards that parents and employers want'. And the mechanism to be used is also clear – the competitive market. Parents must be given more choice, and schools must be encouraged to compete with each other for parents' custom. The icing on the cake is that all this will be done at 'no extra cost to the consumer'.

One apparent contradiction in the 1988 Education Reform Act is that, while much of the Act is concerned with freeing schools from state control, the Act also introduced a highly centralized curriculum and assessment system. The irony of this was not lost on some commentators:

Parents are to be free to choose a school for their children but not free to choose what is taught there, which is the exclusive territory of the Secretary of State. Except for those in the privileged sectors of fee-paying schools and CTCs [City Technology Colleges], freedom of choice over curriculum matters is to be dramatically curtailed for schools, teachers, parents and pupils. The proffered freedom of choice is illusory: parents are free to choose which institution will slavishly teach the Secretary of State's curriculum to their children. (Bash and Coulby, 1989, p. 114)

From the point of view of consumer choice, the introduction of the National Curriculum and standardized assessment does have a certain degree of logic: they provide both the framework for judging schools and the mechanism for making those judgements. If all pupils follow the same curriculum and are assessed against the same benchmarks at the same ages, and if the results of these assessments are then made public, then it will be relatively easy – at least according to theory – for parents to see which are successful schools and which are not. The parents simply consult the local 'league tables' of schools, and make their choices accordingly.

This particular aspect of the reforms was further elaborated by the publication in 1991 of the Parent's Charter (Department of Education and Science, 1991a). This document, which was part of a wider promotion on consumer rights known as the Citizen's Charter, set out the rights and responsibilities expected of parents 'to help you become a more effective partner in your child's education'. Central to the Parent's Charter was 'the right to know', which was enshrined in five key documents:

- an annual written report about each child
- regular reports on schools from independent inspectors
- publicly available 'league tables' comparing the performance of local schools
- a prospectus or brochure about individual schools
- an annual report from each school's governors

The Parent's Charter also spelled out the right of all parents to express their preference for a school of their choice, and their right to appeal if this choice was not met – although it made clear that parents would not automatically get a place in the school of their choice if it was already 'full to capacity with pupils who have a stronger claim'.

The Department of Education and Science intended that the Parent's Charter would be distributed to parents through their children's schools, and no doubt many parents received their copies this way. Some schools and local authorities, however, refused to comply. These objectors pointed out that much of the Parent's Charter contained promises of what the government hoped to introduce in the future, rather than information about what was already enshrined in law. At the time of an imminent general election, they did not wish to be identified with what they saw as a piece of party political electioneering.

The central role of parents in educational reform was emphasized again in another major policy document, the 1992 Education White Paper. Entitled *Choice and Diversity: A New Framework for Schools*, this document made clear that increasing parental choice was one of its main guiding principles. In a passage which has since become widely quoted, the White Paper spelled out its belief that

> Parents know best the needs of their children – certainly better than educational theorists or administrators, better even than our mostly excellent teachers. (p. 2)

Starting from this premise, the White Paper argued for the need to provide as diverse a range of schools as possible, so that parents could choose the school they believed best suited the particular interests and aptitudes of their children. It is clear from reading the White Paper, however, that the authors had a particular type of school in mind which they wished to encourage above all others – grant-maintained schools – and much of the White Paper is in fact concerned with the arrangements necessary to encourage this particular development.

The emphasis on 'diversity' contained in the White Paper has been criticized on the grounds that it is merely another way of talking about inequality in the education system. Brown (1991) argued that it is part of what he calls a 'third wave' in the socio-historical development of British education, a period which he describes by the term 'parentocracy':

> To date, the 'third wave' has been characterised by the rise of the educational *parentocracy*, where a child's education is increasingly dependent upon the *wealth* and *wishes* of parents, rather than the *ability* and *efforts* of pupils. . . . In the educational parentocracy,

selection will be determined by the free play of market forces, and because the State is no longer responsible for overseeing selection, inequalities in educational outcome, at least in official accounts, cannot be blamed on the State. Such inequalities (the Right prefers the term 'diversity') will be viewed as the legitimate expression of parental preferences, differences in innate capacities, and a healthy 'diversity' of educational experience. (pp. 66, 80; emphasis in the original)

We have seen in this section how the new role of parents as consumers emerged from the writings of certain right-wing educationalists in the 1980s, and how it came to play such a central role in the current reforms. We have described the close links between this role and the other main features of the reforms – the National Curriculum, standardized assessment, league tables, diversity and, above all, parental choice. We have also presented some viewpoints which are critical of these developments, on the grounds that they offer illusory freedom and that they will increase rather than reduce educational inequality. It should be pointed out that at this stage such criticisms are purely hypothetical: as with the reforms themselves, it remains to be seen how things will work out in practice.

But what do parents really want?

It might well be assumed that the current reforms – and particularly those aspects which greatly increase the power and influence of parents – arose from a groundswell of popular demand amongst parents for such changes. But in fact, the reality was very different. As we have seen, the idea of giving power to parents arose from the writings of a small but influential group of right-wing educationalists: it did not arise from the parents themselves. Indeed, this point was implicitly made by the Secretary of State for Education, Kenneth Baker, when he told a conference of parents soon after the Education Reform Act was passed:

I have given you more power than you ever had, or ever dreamed of. (cited in Docking, 1990, p. 79)

But even if the reforms were not specifically brought out about by parental demands, it might well be assumed that they are very much in line with what parents actually want. This would certainly seem to be the case if one listens solely to the politicians who have introduced and promoted the reforms: their speeches and writings contain many comments such as 'parents demand higher standards', 'parents want more choice' or 'parents support the National Curriculum'. A typical example came from the Secretary of State for Education, John Patten, when he launched the 1992 White Paper:

Our proposals are radical, sensible and in tune with what parents want. This is above all a common-sense White Paper. (*Times Educational Supplement*, 7 August 1992)

In fact, there is little unequivocal evidence that parents are wholeheartedly in favour of the current reforms. Indeed, if the Scottish experience is of any relevance, there may be some aspects of the reforms which parents are quite unenthusiastic about. In Scotland, where the reforms have taken a somewhat different direction, the proposal to assess all pupils at 8 and 12 years met with strong opposition from both teachers and parents. According to a report in the *Times Educational Supplement*:

The testing policy, pursued vigorously by Michael Forsyth, the right-wing Education Minister, has been overwhelmingly rejected by some 80,000 parents, or three-quarters of parents whose children are eligible for testing. (3 April 1992)

We do not have to look as far afield as Scotland to find evidence that parents do not necessarily agree with all the assumptions underlying the reforms. In March 1989, the Department of Education and Science in England commissioned Public Attitude Surveys Ltd to carry out a large-scale survey of parents' awareness of the current education system and the changes which were about to be introduced. Nearly 2,000 interviews were carried out across the country with the parents of children aged from 5 to 16 years.

The survey showed parents were generally in favour of the proposed changes, although they wanted to know more about what was actually involved. The survey also came up with the revealing finding that 94 per cent of parents were either 'very satisfied' or 'fairly satisfied' with their child's school (Public Attitude Surveys, 1989). This finding, which was not given much publicity at the time, does not fit easily with the idea that parents were so dissatisfied with schools before the reforms were introduced that drastic action was therefore necessary. We shall have more to say about this issue in chapter 6.

We conclude that much of the discussion about the desirability or otherwise of the current reforms has been based more on blanket assertions that they are self-evidently what parents want than on careful research about what parents actually do want. There is little evidence that those who are introducing and implementing the reforms have engaged in any widespread or far-reaching consultations with parents themselves about any aspect of the changes. It is one of the great ironies of the current reforms that, while they have ostensibly been introduced to give parents a greater say in what is happening, they have not been accompanied by a great deal of listening to what parents are actually saying. Indeed, the situation has been succinctly summarized by Duncan Graham, former Chairman of the National Curriculum Council, when he noted that 'Parents are having greatness thrust upon them' (1992, p. 36).

A notorious example of the refusal of Ministers to listen to the views of parents occurred early in 1993, when a group of eight organizations, who between them claimed to represent over 8 million parents, conducted a lobby of MPs at the Houses of Parliament. According to Margaret Morrissey, spokesperson for the National Confederation of Parent–Teacher Associations, these organizations were concerned about the national publication of assessment results which, they felt, 'set school against school and pupil against pupil'. The parents were somewhat upset when the Education Secretary, John Patten, not only refused to see them, but went on BBC Radio Four to say that their views were 'Neanderthal'. Although Mr Patten subsequently published an apology, for many parents the damage had already been done.

Our research: issues and questions

The overriding aim of our research was to go beyond the assertions that the reforms were giving parents what they wanted and
to find out what parents themselves thought about what was
happening to their children's schools. In particular, we wanted to
look not just at what parents felt about the reforms in theory, but
also at how they reacted to them as they unfolded in practice.
This had two immediate implications for the type of research we
needed to do. First, it meant we had to look at parents whose
children were being directly affected by what was going on: this
meant that we needed to study the youngest children in the
education system (Key Stage One, or 5–7 years), as the National
Curriculum and standardized assessment were first introduced
for this age group. Second, it meant we could not just carry out
a 'snap-shot' of parents' views at a particular moment in time:
rather, we had to follow them and their children over a period of
years, as different aspects of the reforms were introduced.

Our interviews with parents focused on six main issues. These
issues will be described briefly here, and then elaborated on when
we discuss our findings. The six issues are all central to the current reforms and bear directly on the assumptions underlying these
innovations.

Issue 1: Parents as consumers   This notion encapsulates the
new role which parents must play if the reforms are to be successful. But it also raises a number of important questions. How far
do parents actually see themselves as consumers? Is it a role with
which they feel comfortable – or even one which they understand? Do their views change over time and, if so, what seems to
underlie such changes? We present our answers to these questions
in chapter 4.

Issue 2: Parental choice   The success of the current reforms
depends crucially on the extent to which parents will choose between schools on the basis of published information about academic performance. But this begs a number of questions. How
do parents actually make choices about their children's schools?

Do they indeed opt primarily for academic factors, or are other aspects of schools more important? What are the constraints on choice – are there some parents who have no realistic choice, or parents who do not consider all the possible choices available to them? We report our findings in chapter 5.

Issue 3: Parental satisfaction   The present reforms rest on the implicit assumption that parents must be dissatisfied with schools as they are now – for if they are not, why bother to make all these changes? We therefore look in chapter 6 at how far parents can be described as 'dissatisfied customers'. We start by asking what criteria the parents adopted when judging schools. We then look at whether they were happy with their children's current school, and whether they thought the teachers were doing a good job. We ask whether some parents were so dissatisfied that they actually moved their children to another school and, if so, what made them do this. Finally, we compare parents' feelings about their children's school with their concerns about 'standards' more generally.

Issue 4: Parents and the National Curriculum   It is widely assumed that parents are favourably disposed towards the National Curriculum, but this assumption has rarely been tested in practice. In chapter 7 we look at whether parents approve of the National Curriculum, whether they are happy with the priority given to English, maths and science within the National Curriculum, and what they think should be taught within these subjects. We also look at whether parents think it is appropriate that the foundation subjects – such as history, geography and technology – should be introduced to children at this stage.

Issue 5: Parents' knowledge about school   Our starting point here is the assumption that the current reforms will make a substantial difference to parents' knowledge about what is happening to their children in school. In chapter 8, we put this assumption to the test. We look at the extent of parents' knowledge in a number of areas, including what they know about the current reforms, about what their children are learning, and about their children's progress. We ask whether the parents are happy with their current levels of knowledge, and examine the ways in which they are currently obtaining information about what goes on at school.

Issue 6: Parents and assessment   The standardized assessment of all children at the age of 7 years has been vigorously promoted on the grounds that it will raise educational standards and that it is widely supported by parents. In chapter 9 we look at how far these assumptions are true. The parents in our study have a particularly valuable perspective to offer, for their children were among the first cohort of 7-year-olds ever to be assessed under the new arrangements. We look at how the assessments were experienced by the children and their parents, and ask what the parents actually learnt from the whole exercise. We also look at the parents' attitudes to various aspects of the assessment process, and at how their attitudes were changed by their own direct experience of assessment.

Before presenting our findings, we make two small but important diversions. In chapter 2 we present the views of another group who are centrally involved in the current reforms – the headteachers of primary schools. We look at how these headteachers see the parents with whom they are currently dealing, focusing specifically on the six issues outlined above. As we will see, the views of these headteachers form an important backcloth against which the views of parents can be contrasted.

The second diversion is to explain in more detail how we actually carried out our research with parents. In chapter 3 we briefly describe how we selected our sample, the ways in which it changed over time, how the interviews were carried out, and what we did with the data collected. We also address the important question of whether the parents' involvement in the research had a significant effect on their own thinking and behaviour.

Overview

In this chapter we have focused on the central role which parents are required to play in the current educational reforms – that of consumers of education. We have contrasted this role with two other ways in which parents are frequently perceived – as partners and as problems. We have described how the emphasis on parents as consumers arose from a particular political perspective, and how it came to underpin the current reforms. We have argued that this new role has been handed to parents with little or no consultation. Our research, in contrast, is an attempt to find out what parents really want, and how they are reacting as the reforms unfold in practice.

2
How Headteachers See Parents

> If I produced sausages I suppose I would see parents as consumers, but at the moment I see them as people becoming more aware and more interested. I see them as partners rather than consumers.
>
> *(Headteacher's comment)*

In the last chapter we described some of the different ways in which parents are seen by politicians and educationalists. In this chapter we look at how parents are perceived by headteachers. These perceptions come from a series of telephone interviews we carried out with a sample of primary headteachers during the course of our study. As will be seen, the views of these headteachers provide an illuminating contrast with the views of the parents themselves.

One of the main reasons for focusing on headteachers comes from the central role they play in shaping the relationship between a school and its parents. For example, when prospective parents first come to look at a school, the headteacher is likely to be the person who meets them and shows them round; when newsletters or reports are sent home from school, the head's name is usually the one at the bottom of the page; and if problems arise with their child, then the head will often be the person whom parents approach to sort things out. The head's attitude towards parents, and the way he or she deals with such encounters, is thus likely to have a crucial effect on how parents see the school. In addition, the head's attitude to parents can strongly influence the way other teachers in the school relate to parents, so that a distinctive approach to parents can develop and permeate throughout the whole school.

The central importance of the headteacher's role in dealing with parents has been heightened by the current reforms. The devolvement of financial management to schools means that the head now has particular responsibility for balancing the budget and maintaining pupil numbers. Heads are thus under increasing pressure to promote their school in the community and to compete with other local schools for the custom of parents. In short, the headteacher is in a critical position to provide valuable insights into how the reforms are affecting the relationship between parents and schools.

Despite the central role which headteachers play in home/school relationships, there has been little previous research on how heads perceive parents. Indeed, the most recent study is probably one published in 1979 by Cyster, Clift and Battle, which contains a chapter on headteachers' perceptions of parental involvement. We therefore felt it was timely to look at how headteachers see parents in the current educational climate.

The headteachers

At the start of the study we wrote to every fourth primary school in a single local authority in the southwest of England. This authority covers a large and diverse area, and the schools varied widely on factors such as their size, locality and the socio-economic make-up of their catchment areas. The headteachers were asked if they would be willing to take part in a short telephone interview about parents and the National Curriculum. A few heads refused on the grounds that they were too busy actually implementing the National Curriculum to talk about it, but the great majority agreed to take part. We contacted the heads again a year later for a follow-up interview, and then contacted them a year after that for a final interview. While there were inevitably some changes to the sample as headteachers retired or moved on, we were nevertheless still able to interview between 70 and 80 headteachers each year.

The interviews took between 15 and 45 minutes, and focused on the six main issues outlined at the end of chapter 1. More specifically, the headteachers were asked:

- how far they saw their parents as consumers
- how far their school was affected by increased parental choice
- what their parents thought 'makes a good school'
- whether their parents seemed satisfied with the school
- how much their parents knew about the National Curriculum and standardized assessment
- whether their parents approved or disapproved of the National Curriculum and standardized assessment

While the main focus of these questions was on parents, our interviews inevitably revealed the huge amount of pressure which many headteachers were experiencing. It was clear that their job had become much more difficult and complex over the previous few years, and this was reflected more than anything in the vast increase in official forms and documents which they were encountering. Many heads voiced their concern that the time they could spend teaching children was decreasing as the amount of administration increased. These pressures were felt most acutely by teaching heads in small schools, and the few heads who were too busy to take part in our survey came mainly from this category. Other heads pointed to the increased stress and work-load amongst their staff caused by the reforms, while one or two seemed on the point of going under themselves! Nevertheless, we were always impressed by the willingness with which the heads were prepared to put aside the many other demands on their time and take part in our interviews.

Parents as consumers

Each year the headteachers were asked how far they saw their parents as consumers. Their replies were assigned to one of three main categories – 'very much so', 'to some extent' and 'not at all'.

Table 2.1 How far do headteachers see parents as consumers?

	Year 1 (n = 81)	Year 2 (n = 71)	Year 3 (n = 78)
Very much so	36%	35%	38%
To some extent	38%	41%	37%
Not at all	26%	24%	24%

The proportion of headteachers responding each year in each category is shown in table 2.1. This table shows a very consistent pattern over the three years of the study. About three-quarters of the headteachers said each year that they saw their parents as consumers, to some extent at least, while about a quarter of the heads said they did not. Those in the former group typically justified their answers by pointing out that times were changing, and that parents were increasingly to be seen in economic terms. This point was made by different headteachers in different ways:

> They're very much consumers. Without them we'd be out of a job.

> Yes, they carry pockets of money. Each child taken away is £70. You've got to see children leaving as finance going out of the door.

> Whatever we're trying to establish in school we have to recognise that parents are money-bearers. They have the right to go elsewhere, and the money goes with them, so tough for us.

But alongside this widespread recognition of the new market era, there was also a frequently expressed distaste for the whole discourse of consumerism and market forces. Many heads commented that they did not like the term 'consumer' and the approach to education that it embodied. Such comments were made both by heads who saw parents as consumers and by those who did not. For example, the headteacher of a small village school expressed her personal dislike for this way of seeing parents alongside a clear statement that she was in fact attempting to provide what parents wanted:

> I don't really like to look at it that way. But they are consumers.
> We offer a service and they object if it's not the quality they like,
> so we try to give them that service.

Other heads were opposed both to the notion of consumerism and to putting the idea into practice. The following comment was made by the head of a school which had a good reputation and where numbers were rising. He showed little sign of compromising with what he felt he should be providing in the school:

> It's not a term to use in children's education. I would not want
> parents if they didn't like the style of education on offer. Education
> is too organic to be thought of in consumer terms.

Several heads commented that they saw the *children* as consumers, not their parents. This did not seem to be merely a rhetorical point, but rather reflected these heads' beliefs about whom education was ultimately for. They saw their business as primarily concerned with helping children learn, and only secondarily, if at all, with parents' rights as consumers. This position was expressed particularly strongly by the following head:

> Clearly in my mind children are consumers. The Government were
> wrong to produce a Parent's Charter – it should be a Children's
> Charter, containing a right to reasonably-sized classes, adequate
> facilities and so on. Every child should have the same rights, they
> should not be differentiated between first and second class.

Many of the heads spontaneously commented that they saw parents primarily as *partners*. Interestingly, this comment was made both by heads who said they saw parents as consumers and by heads who did not. The following head, for example, said that she saw parents very much as consumers, but that this was by no means incompatible with seeing them as partners:

> Yes, I do see them as consumers. They're actively involved in the
> life of the school. It's a partnership in which we are mindful of

their desires. They're kept fully informed of what's happening in the school.

In contrast, other heads expressed a clear distinction between seeing parents as consumers and seeing them as partners. This point was graphically made by the head of a small rural school:

> If I produced sausages I suppose I would see parents as consumers, but at the moment I see them as people becoming more aware and more interested. I see them as partners rather than consumers.

These comments suggest that for many heads the perception of parents as partners had some sort of priority in their thinking. For these heads, it seemed unlikely that their perception of parents as partners would simply be replaced by a new perception of parents as consumers. Rather, it appeared that the idea of partnership would have to be reworked to fit in with the realities of the new educational climate. From this point of view, the following head's comments are particularly revealing. She was in charge of the only school for children aged 5–7 years in a small rural town. In the first interview, she anticipated that she was about to embark on a process of rethinking. Two years later, the process was apparently under way – although, in her mind, there was still some reworking to be done:

Year 1   They are consumers, but I haven't really changed my thinking on it yet. But I'm beginning to do so.

Year 3   I see them much more as consumers. I see we've got to provide what they require. We have to provide them with as much information as possible. Although we're not dealing with a consumable thing at the end of the day, we still have to rethink lots of our words.

Asking headteachers how far they saw parents as consumers had raised a number of interesting issues. Although the heads were acutely aware of the new economic order in which they were operating, there was clearly some reluctance to embrace it whole-heartedly. The idea that education was primarily for children's benefit, and that parents should be seen primarily as partners, appeared to be widely held. It remains to be seen how far this perception of parents as partners can fit alongside the newer perception of parents as consumers.

The effects of increased parental choice

Closely related to the issue of parents as consumers is that of increased parental choice. As we saw in chapter 1, it is a central assumption of the current reforms that parents will make considered choices between schools on the basis of publicly available information, and that schools will therefore have to compete more vigorously with each other for parents' custom. In order to find out how this was working out in practice, we asked the headteachers each year how concerned they were about parents sending their children elsewhere. We also asked them if increased parental choice was affecting their schools in any other way.

Despite their comments about the new economic climate, the majority of heads did not seem too concerned about prospective parents going elsewhere (see table 2.2). Various reasons were given for this apparent lack of concern. One of the most common was that their schools were popular with parents, and in some cases were already full or over-subscribed. The headteacher of one such school said that he was 'delighted' if parents sent their children elsewhere, while other headteachers described how they were having to operate selection policies to keep their numbers within manageable limits. These headteachers, in other words, were

Table 2.2 How concerned are headteachers about prospective parents going elsewhere?

	Year 1 (n = 83)	Year 2 (n = 71)	Year 3 (n = 79)
Very concerned	2%	4%	8%
Some concern	22%	28%	30%
Not concerned	76%	68%	62%

operating in a sellers' rather than a buyers' market: instead of parents choosing schools, the schools were effectively choosing their parents.

Another reason given for their lack of concern about losing parents was that for many parents there were no realistic alternatives to the present school. In some cases there was no other school in the area, while in other cases the alternative schools were full. Several headteachers noted that the choices available to parents were severely limited by transport problems. For example, the head of a small isolated rural school pointed out that

> There's very little choice, in that there's no public transport. And there's no pavements on many of these roads. The next school is 4 miles away, you need a car to get there.

There was a small but growing minority of headteachers who did express their concern about prospective parents going elsewhere (see table 2.2). Some of these heads seemed resigned to losing custom. One head, for example, talked about how it was the historical tradition in her town for middle-class families to attend a different school, and she could see little possibility of getting them to come to her school. Several heads mentioned the problem of how schools acquired a certain reputation amongst parents, which was not always accurate, but which was often extremely hard to overcome. A graphic illustration of this point was provided by a headteacher who overheard two parents discussing his school at the hairdressers, without their realizing that he was listening:

> One of them said 'I don't like that school, I don't like that school, and as for (the head's) school, I wouldn't send a dog there'. It's the social perception within the town. It's seen as rough, with parents who are bad tenants. It's very hard to attract people from outside.

Other heads were taking active steps to win back parents. One headteacher described how her school was deliberately building up its nursery provision in order to make the school more attractive to prospective parents. This head made clear that she was getting little official support for the policy, but felt she was forced to follow it in order not to lose custom:

We'll get no more money from the LEA, but we've got to try to attract them in. If another nursery that has spaces gets them in there they stay with that school.

Many heads commented that parents were increasingly likely to visit a number of schools and make explicit comparisons before coming to a decision. Several of these heads were critical of parents who did this, for a number of reasons. One head of a very small rural school seemed strongly opposed to the whole idea of parental choice:

I don't want parents who are so fussy, who go around comparing schools. Parents who do so are stupid. If something's wrong with the local school they should stick with it and change it from within.

Other heads were not quite so negative about the principle of parental choice, but expressed their concerns about the criteria that parents might use in coming to their decision:

I'm concerned at how parents choose. I'm anxious that parents are not choosing as they should, but for futile reasons rather than sound educational reasons.

Some heads felt that parents were becoming increasingly aware of their power and that schools were being put under increasing pressure by parental demands. One head described how some parents were now asking not just for a place at the school, but for a place in a particular class. Another reported that parents were more likely to appeal if their child was not given a place in the school, and were increasingly winning such appeals. As a result, class sizes in her school were rising to what she felt was an unacceptable level. However, there were also many heads who commented more on the apathy of their parents than on their militancy. As one head pointedly remarked:

I'm under more pressure from central government than from any of my parents.

These responses make clear that the effects of increased parental choice vary considerably from school to school. A minority of schools seemed to be in danger of losing parents' custom beyond the point at which they would cease to be viable; their heads were responding to this danger in ways that ranged from entrepreneurialism to resignation. The majority of heads, however, were operating in a sellers' market and were relatively unaffected by increased parental choice: these heads seemed to be well insulated from the realities of the new educational market.

How do parents judge schools?

In the course of answering questions about increased parental choice, several headteachers expressed their concerns about how parents judge schools. This concern was expressed particularly clearly by the headteacher who commented that parents were choosing for 'futile reasons rather than sound educational reasons'. We probed further into this issue in Year 3 by asking the headteachers what they thought parents valued in a school. Specifically, we asked them 'what do you think parents think makes a good school?' The wording of the question was deliberately chosen to be identical with a question we asked the parents themselves (see chapter 6). The heads' responses were assigned to particular categories, and these are shown in table 2.3. The percentages add up to more than 100 per cent, as most of the heads mentioned more than one factor.

The headteachers mentioned a wide range of factors which they felt were important to parents when judging a school (see table 2.3). Of these, the most frequently mentioned factor was that parents judged a school primarily in terms of their own child's happiness. Several heads explicitly remarked that parents placed more emphasis on their child's happiness than on academic results, and this was supported by the relatively small number of heads who mentioned the latter factor. As the head of a large inner-city school put it:

Parents here first and foremost like to see their children happy. I think that parents more generally would be looking at the breadth of curriculum, and at the quality of teaching and learning opportunities, but that's probably *not* the case with our parents. For them happiness is the most important criterion.

The heads' belief that parents placed greatest value on what might be termed 'non-academic' factors also emerged in the relatively high frequency with which criteria such as the school's 'ethos', 'discipline', 'atmosphere' and 'relationships' were cited. One aspect of ethos which was mentioned particularly frequently was the way in which parents were regarded by the school:

They like the fact that we have time to listen to them and their children. That we try to communicate and inform them right across the board, whether it's about social events, sporting activities, or the curriculum.

While heads felt that parents put priority on non-academic matters, children's progress and learning were not ignored. Over a third of the heads thought that parents judged a school by the progress their children were making, and a similar proportion mentioned that parents valued a traditional approach to education.

Table 2.3 Headteachers' views on what parents think makes a good school (Year 3, *n* = 78)

Own child happy	56%
Ethos	40%
Traditional education	37%
Progress/standards	36%
Discipline	28%
Relationships	26%
Atmosphere	20%
Image	17%
Wide-ranging education	15%
Pastoral	11%
Working ethic	9%
Academic results	8%
The head	4%
The staff	3%

These heads felt that parents judged a school by the emphasis it gave to teaching basic skills – particularly reading – and to the use of more formal teaching methods:

> Some parents just want reading, writing and arithmetic. It was good enough for them, and they think it should be good enough for their children.

Very few heads mentioned the staff or the head as being important factors for parents. This may have been a genuine perception of how the parents saw them, but it could also have been that the heads were simply too modest to suggest to an outsider that they were the most crucial part of a school. Indeed, such modesty was explicitly mentioned by one of the few heads who referred to her own role:

> I'm a teaching head and so I'm seen by a lot of the children and parents. It all goes to make a happy school. Am I being big-headed in saying it's something to do with me?

The possibility that parents might place more value on their children's happiness than on academic results represents a significant problem for the current reforms. As we saw in chapter 1, the reforms rest heavily on the assumption that parents will choose between schools on the basis of published information about academic performance. However, if the heads are right and parents are more interested in their children's happiness than in academic success, they may well choose a school which happens to have poorer published results if they think their child might be happier there. We will pursue this issue further in chapters 5 and 6, when we look at the criteria which parents actually employ for choosing and evaluating schools.

Parents' satisfaction with the school

Another assumption underlying the current reforms is that parents are generally dissatisfied with schools as they are now – for if they are not, then what is the need for reform? In order to find out how far this assumption was shared by the headteachers, we asked them how satisfied they thought their parents were with the school. We also asked them if their parents had any concerns about 'standards' in education more generally.

The headteachers were virtually unanimous in saying that their parents were either 'satisfied' or 'very satisfied' with the school. Not a single headteacher in any year thought their parents were dissatisfied, although there were one or two heads who said they were not sure or that they didn't know. Typically, the headteachers justified their answers by saying that 'no-one complains' or that 'the feedback is positive'. As the head of a popular urban first school put it:

> They manifestly are satisfied. They keep coming here, and they don't come complaining. My business is to chat them up when they're in school. I've always been into PR. My philosophy is that if we don't hang together we hang separately, and the poor kid will end up in the middle.

The headteachers' perception that their parents were 'manifestly satisfied' with the school does not fit easily with the assumption of widespread parental dissatisfaction with schools. It is possible, of course, that even if the headteachers felt there was substantial dissatisfaction at their school they would be unlikely to reveal this to a comparative stranger over the telephone (or as Mandy Rice-Davies once put it, 'they would say that, wouldn't they?'). Another possibility is that there actually was considerable parental dissatisfaction in these schools but the heads were simply not aware of it: the parents may have felt unable or unwilling to share their feelings with the school. Yet another possibility is that the heads were accurate in their perceptions of parents' views, and that the idea of widespread parental dissatisfaction is itself a myth. We shall discuss this further in chapter 6 when we look at what the parents themselves said about their children's schools.

A different perspective on this issue came when we asked the heads whether their parents had wider concerns about 'standards' in education. Just over half the heads (56 per cent) replied that their parents did not seem to have such concerns. These heads typically pointed out that their parents were mostly concerned with their own child's progress, that they seemed to be happy with what was happening at the school, and that they had received no complaints or negative feedback. However, just over a quarter of the heads (26 per cent) felt that their parents had wider concerns about standards, particularly in the area of reading, although they were not necessarily concerned about standards at their own child's school.

Many of the heads felt that the media played a leading part in generating parental concerns about standards, and that it was their role as headteachers to attempt to counteract what parents had been told. Some of the heads talked vividly in terms of 'a battle for parents' minds', and described various methods which they used to combat the influence of the media. The most common approach was to demonstrate to parents what was really going on in the school, either through open evenings where the school's teaching methods were explained, or through displays, or through inviting parents in to look round. The theme of the school battling against the media to influence parents' beliefs was one which recurred frequently in these interviews with headteachers.

Parents' knowledge about the National Curriculum and assessment

The headteachers thought that parents had only a limited amount of knowledge about the National Curriculum and its associated assessment procedures. Not surprisingly, this view was particularly prevalent at the start of the study, when the National Curriculum had only just been introduced and when little was known about how the assessments would actually be carried out. Several heads felt that parents had been actively misinformed by the media at this stage:

They read the papers and think it's all up and running.

Virtually all the heads said they were attempting to inform parents about the National Curriculum, using methods such as

Table 2.4 Headteachers' views on whether parents want to know
more about the National Curriculum

	Year 1 (n = 83)	Year 2 (n = 71)	Year 3 (n = 79)
Parents do	24%	14%	15%
Parents don't	48%	54%	54%
Parents differ	24%	24%	28%
Don't know	4%	8%	3%

sending home newsletters and leaflets, holding meetings or dis-
playing National Curriculum materials on classroom walls. One
school described in some detail how the governing body had set
up working parties on each subject, and the working parties
reported regularly in the local village newspaper. In spite of such
efforts, however, the great majority of heads still felt that their
parents were not very well informed. As one head commented in
the Year 3 interview:

> They're getting more and more knowledgeable because of what
> teachers are doing. But there's still an awful lot of ignorance. I was
> talking recently to one parent who's the manager of the local shop.
> He thinks the National Curriculum is like a training manual – it
> tells you exactly what to do.

The headteachers were asked each year if they thought their
parents wanted to know more about the National Curriculum. As
can be seen from table 2.4, the most common response was that
they did not. About a quarter of heads pointed out that parents
differed in this respect, although many added that those parents
who wanted to know more were usually a small minority. Typical
responses to this question were that parents were 'not interested',
'not bothered' or in some cases 'apathetic'. Many parents were
seen as having little interest in what went on at school as long as
their own children were happy. Sometimes this was put more
positively in terms of parents trusting the teachers, or being content

to leave the complexities of the job to the professionals. As one head put it:

> As long as they have confidence in the school and the staff, they will be happy and will realise we're doing a job. They will show supportive interest. But they won't take over.

The heads often justified their belief that parents did not want to know more by pointing to the poor take-up of attempts to keep parents informed. Several heads remarked that there had been a low turn-out for evening meetings organized to inform parents about the curriculum – in some cases only a handful of parents had turned up – or predicted that such meetings would be poorly attended. The headteacher of a large primary school with a middle-class catchment area on the edge of a big city commented that

> If we ran a meeting it would be good if 50 out of 500 came, and even then only half a dozen would take on board what we were really saying.

Other heads provided different sorts of evidence for parental lack of interest in the National Curriculum.

> The PTA committee was asked in the summer term if they wanted a talk about the National Curriculum. They laughed! They said they wanted something more interesting. It wasn't very positive.

> They couldn't be bothered. We had large numbers of glossy DES publications. They were thrown away as parents didn't ask for them.

> I offered one mum the National Curriculum folder. She said she couldn't read all that – she much prefers what she reads in the paper.

While the headteachers mostly considered that parents did not *want* to know more about the National Curriculum, there was general agreement that parents *needed* to know more (see table 2.5). This response was frequently supported by comments that parents

Table 2.5 Headteachers' views on whether parents need to know more about the National Curriculum

	Year 1 (n = 82)	Year 2 (n = 68)	Year 3 (n = 78)
Parents do	86%	77%	73%
Parents don't	6%	19%	14%
Parents differ	1%	0%	0%
Mixed feelings	7%	4%	13%

needed to update their views on education, as these were often based on their own experience of education or on what they heard from the media. As one head rather despairingly put it:

> They believe the *Daily Mail* more than the stuff that comes home from school.

Several heads commented that the more informed their parents were, the better able they would be to help their child, or to help the teachers help their child. At the same time, it was often pointed out that there were limits to what the school could be expected to do to inform parents, as well as to the amount of knowledge it would be useful for parents to have. The comment that 'a little knowledge is a dangerous thing', or some variant on that theme, was frequently made:

> If they needed to know more they would have asked, though they may be head-in-sandish. It's always desirable to know more, as a little knowledge can be a dangerous thing, but there's a limit to the time we can spend.

> It's a difficult question. There must be a happy medium. Too much knowledge can be unhelpful or confusing. Lay people may not understand everything – it may simply cause worry.

Asking the headteachers about the nature and extent of parental knowledge had produced a clear consensus in their replies.

Parents were generally seen as having limited knowledge about the current reforms and as not *wanting* to know any more. At the same time, most heads felt that parents *needed* to know more about these developments, although there were limits to the amount of knowledge which was seen as desirable. It was not clear from the heads' replies how information should best be transmitted to parents. While the heads clearly felt this should not be left to the media, there were doubts about the effectiveness of the methods commonly used by schools – such as evening meetings, leaflets, or making information available at the school. We shall return to these issues in chapter 8, when we look at them from the parents' perspective.

Parents' attitude to the National Curriculum and assessment

The majority of headteachers believed that their parents approved of the National Curriculum, and they were increasingly likely to say this as the study wore on (see table 2.6). Typically, the heads justified their response by saying that parents thought it would improve standards – either in their child's own school or in the country at large.

Table 2.6 Headteachers' views on whether parents approve or disapprove of the National Curriculum

	Year 1 (n = 82)	Year 2 (n = 70)	Year 3 (n = 79)
Parents approve	38%	54%	72%
Parents have mixed feelings	20%	6%	6%
Parents disapprove	2%	4%	3%
Parents have no opinion	14%	17%	9%
Parents differ	9%	4%	5%
Don't know how parents feel	17%	14%	5%

While most of the heads believed that parents approved of the National Curriculum, they often seemed reluctant to accept that parents might have come to this opinion through their own devices. Instead, they frequently referred to ways in which parents might have been 'influenced' by one source or another. The two sources of influence which were most frequently mentioned were the media and the school itself:

> They've been told by the media it's a good thing.

> They approve because they've been told that it will get rid of bad teachers.

> We've made sure they approve because we're approving too.

Some heads commented that parents did not know enough about the National Curriculum to have an opinion, while others referred again to indifference or apathy on the parents' part:

> As long as their child is happy and progressing, it makes no difference if it's the National Curriculum or not.

or, more bluntly,

> They couldn't be bothered.

Although the headteachers were increasingly sure that their parents approved of the National Curriculum, they were much less certain about whether parents approved of assessment. Each year only a minority of heads were prepared to commit themselves to a clear statement about parents' attitude, with the rest saying that they didn't know what parents thought, that parents differed, that parents had mixed feelings, or that parents had no opinion. As before, there was a widespread feeling that parents were likely to have been influenced by the media or the school in coming to their opinion:

> There's general disapproval – it comes from the school.

There's a tendency to follow the media influence, so a minority think it's more important than it is.

Overview

The headteachers whom we interviewed were doing their best to cope with a huge amount of externally generated change. A key component in this change is that parents need to be perceived in a different light – not as problems or as partners, but as consumers. How, then, did this group of headteachers see their parents?

Clearly, there is not a simple answer to this question. As we have seen, there was considerable variation amongst the headteachers in how they perceived their parents. While we have not explored this variation systematically, it appears to reflect a variety of factors, such as differences in the school's place in the educational market, in the nature of its catchment area, and in the head's own particular approach to education. Yet despite this variation in the headteachers' views, there were three broad themes which emerged from what they were saying.

First, there appeared to be clear limits in the extent to which parents were actually seen as 'consumers'. While the majority of heads undoubtedly said that they saw parents as consumers, at least to some extent, this perception was frequently qualified. Many heads said they disliked the term and its connotations, or that they would rather see children as consumers, or that they preferred to think of parents as 'partners'. At the same time, only a minority of heads were concerned about losing their parents' custom: the majority were operating in a sellers' market, and in some cases were the only stallholders in sight. Our overall impression was that many heads were paying little more than lip-service to the notion of parents as consumers: in reality, they had not yet experienced the full force of a competitive market.

Second, parents were frequently seen as having a very narrow set of concerns in relation to schools. If their own children were happy – and the heads were virtually unanimous in thinking they were – then the parents were mostly content to let the school get on with the job. Phrases like 'not interested', 'not bothered' or 'apathetic' were common. Naturally, there were some parents who did not fit this stereotype – those who attended meetings or who asked awkward questions – but these were usually portrayed as a 'vocal minority' who contrasted strongly with the 'silent majority'. It should be noted that if this perception of widespread apathy amongst parents is accurate, then it does not bode well for the current reforms: a population of disinterested and contented parents is hardly likely to provide the driving force for radical change.

Finally, the headteachers frequently portrayed parents as being easily influenced by outside agencies. The most prominent agency in this respect was the media, which was often seen as shaping parents' views on issues such as declining standards in reading or the desirability of the National Curriculum. At the same time, many heads felt that the schools themselves could have a strong influence on parents' views, and some heads even talked in terms of a 'battle for parents' minds' between the media and themselves. The idea that parents might have distinct and carefully thought-out views of their own was not prominent amongst the head-teachers' replies.

The evidence from these first two chapters suggests that there are a number of important differences – as well as similarities – between the ways in which parents are perceived by headteachers and the way they have been described by politicians and educationalists. It is now time to turn to the parents themselves, and find out how they see the current reforms.

3

Interviewing Parents

I feel the interviews are a support and a chance to bounce ideas off you. It's a great feeling referring back to what I said a year ago. It'll be a disgrace if this research stops – it should be carried on all the way through.

(Parent's comments on being interviewed)

The main aim of our research was to obtain the thoughts, feelings and perceptions of a group of parents who were directly affected by the current educational reforms. It was clear from the start that the only way we could do this was by carrying out in-depth interviews with the parents in their own homes. Alternative methods, such as asking parents to complete questionnaires or interviewing them at school, would certainly have been more convenient for us, but they were quickly discarded on the grounds that they would provide neither the depth nor the candour which we required. Nevertheless, we still had a number of methodological problems to solve. How could we minimize the problem of parents moving away or otherwise leaving the sample? Should we aim to interview the father, the mother or both parents together? How could we ensure that our sample was not biased in one direction or another? Should we use a tape-recorder, or try to write down everything as it was said? In this chapter we describe how we tackled these and other methodological problems: readers who are more interested in our findings might wish to skim the chapter or omit it altogether.

Selecting parents

Because of the time involved in carrying out and analysing in-depth interviews, we estimated that the maximum sample size would have to be somewhere between 120 and 150 families. As we had limited funds for travel, it was clear that all the families would have to be located in the southwest of England, within reasonable distance of our base in Exeter.

We used the telephone interviews with primary headteachers (described in chapter 2) as the first step in selecting parents. In the course of these interviews we obtained information from the heads about the size of their school, the nature of its catchment area and their willingness to participate further in our study. From this initial sample of 83 schools we selected 11 schools who formed the core schools in the study. These 11 schools were carefully chosen so that they varied according to their size (small, medium or large), their locality (urban, small town or rural) and the socio-economic nature of their catchment area (middle-class, working-class or mixed). One school was for infants only (4–7 years) while the remainder were combined infant/junior schools (4–11 years).

The schools also varied according to the way the headteachers described their parents. One school, for example, was located in a small village which served a widely scattered catchment area: here the parents were said to take little interest in the school and hankered after a return to traditional methods. Another school was situated in a desirable residential area in a locality which still retained the 11-plus: here the parents were seen as being highly competitive individuals who subjected the school – and their children – to a great deal of pressure. A third school was located in a run-down inner-city neighbourhood: here the parents were seen as being apathetic and preoccupied with their own problems.

Having chosen our schools, we wrote individual letters to the parents of all children at the start of Year 1 (5–6 years) at each school, except that in the three largest schools we only used children from one class in that year group. Our letter explained that we were carrying out research on parents' views about the National Curriculum, and that we would like to interview them in their own homes. The letter gave parents the opportunity to decline if they so wished. Of the 163 families who received this initial letter, ten chose not to be involved, and a further four parents could not be contacted at all. We also found that 11 children whose names had been given to us by their school were in fact too old to be assessed at the same time as the other children, and so these children were dropped from the study. This left us with an initial sample of 138 families.

Changes to the sample over time

It is inevitable with research of this nature that the sample will get smaller as the study proceeds. Families may move out of the area, their circumstances may change so they are no longer available for further interviews, or the novelty of being in a research study may wear off. In fact, we were pleasantly surprised by the relatively small number of parents who were lost to the research: over the entire period of the study, only 12 families either moved away or could not be contacted again. This undoubtedly reflects the fact that the southwest has a relatively stable population compared with other parts of the country. But it also reflects the fact that the overwhelming majority of parents found the interviews both enjoyable and relevant to their lives.

Figure 3.1 shows in more detail what happened to the sample over the three years of the project. At the top of the figure are the 138 families who were interviewed in Year 1. In the period between the Year 1 and Year 2 interviews, five families left the area altogether: this was usually because of changes to the father's job, although in one case we were told that the parents had separated and the mother had gone off to Spain. Three further families were 'not contactable' when we tried to arrange the interviews in Year 2. In one case the mother had left home and the father did not reply to our requests for an interview; in another case the parents had also separated and we were advised by the school not to pursue them as the situation was extremely fraught, while in the third case the family simply disappeared from their temporary accommodation and were never seen again.

A further seven children moved to new schools between Year 1

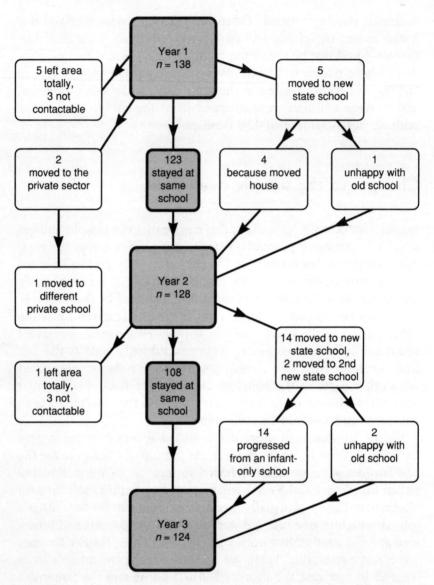

Figure 3.1   Changes in sample over the three years of the project.

and Year 2. Five of these children went to different schools in the state sector; in four cases this was because the family moved house, while in one case the parents were unhappy with the previous school. In addition, two children moved out of the state sector into private schools. We continued to interview the parents of all seven of these children, and in chapter 6 we will look more closely at why they moved their children from one school to another. However, as the two children who went into private schools did not experience the National Curriculum or standardized assessment, the interviews with their parents were rather different, and their data were excluded from most of our analyses.

Between Years 2 and 3 of the project we lost one more family who moved out of the area, and a further three families who were 'not contactable' in Year 3. One of these parents was always out when we arrived to interview her: she finally left us a message on her front door saying 'sorry out – children settled in new school fine'. Another parent was under considerable duress during Year 2 as her elder son had been killed in a car accident: understandably, she did not feel like talking to us in Year 3. The third parent simply defied all attempts to contact her: she was not on the phone and was either out or refused to answer the door whenever we called.

In addition, 16 children moved to other state schools between Years 2 and 3. This number, which at first sight seems surprisingly large, is explained by the fact that 14 of these children attended an 'infants only' school and so had to move schools anyway at the end of Year 2. All these children moved on to the nearest junior school. Two further children, both of whom had moved to new state schools between Years 1 and 2, moved on to different state schools. No children moved into the private sector during the second year of the project, although one child moved from one private school to another.

Which parent was interviewed

One important decision we had to make was whether to interview both parents in each family, or only one. To a large extent this was decided for us: we simply did not have the resources to interview both parents on each occasion and carry out the subsequent analysis of their data. But other factors were involved as well. It was inevitable that we would get similar answers from both parents to some questions (which is not to say that they would necessarily agree on everything) and so their data could not be treated as independent in any subsequent analysis. Further, we were not sure how we would cope with the practical difficulties of ensuring that two separate interviews took place in the same household at the same time: we felt rather uncomfortable at the thought of sending one parent out of the room while we interviewed the other. We therefore decided to interview only one parent in each family: at the same time, we decided not to object if the other parent wanted to be present during the interview.

The decision to interview only one parent raised the question of whether this would be the mother or the father. Our solution was to let individual families make this decision for us. In other words, we made it clear to each family when setting up the first interview that we wanted to interview one of the parents, but that it was up to them to choose which one. In practice, we usually ended up interviewing the parent who was most available during the day-time or early evening – our normal interviewing times. This also had the advantage that we were usually interviewing the parent who had most day-to-day contact with the school. Having established who would be interviewed on the first occasion, our aim on subsequent occasions was to re-interview the same parent as far as possible.

Table 3.1 shows which parent, or combination of parents, was interviewed each year. As can be seen, we usually interviewed the mother on her own, but sometimes it was the father alone. On some occasions both parents were interviewed together: when this happened, one of the parents tended to answer most of the questions, and it was this parent's answers which were analysed, although sometimes the parents agreed on a joint answer. On other occasions, one parent was interviewed while the other parent (or another partner) was present in the room but played little part in the interview.

Table 3.1 Parent interviewed on each occasion

	Year 1	Year 2	Year 3
Mother alone	112	103	100
Father alone	10	11	9
Mother and father together	4	6	6
Mother (with father present)	2	5	6
Father (with mother present)	8	3	3
Mother (with other partner present)	2	0	0
Father (with other partner present)	0	0	0
Total	138	128	124

Table 3.2 Socio-economic status of initial parent sample

Professional	33	24%
Intermediate	18	13%
Skilled non-manual	30	22%
Skilled manual	11	8%
Semi-skilled	19	14%
Unskilled	22	16%
Parent	5	4%
Total	138	100%

The nature of the sample

In order to make sure that our sample contained parents with a wide range of socio-economic backgrounds, we enquired of each parent interviewed about their current or most recent occupation. This was then categorized according to the Registrar General's (1981) classification system, one of the most widely used systems of its kind. The results of this categorization are shown in table 3.2.

These categories themselves contained a wide range of occupations. Thus the 'professional' category included teachers,

lecturers, nurses, solicitors and a dentist; the 'intermediate' category included parents who owned their own businesses, such as
hairdressing and catering, as well those who worked in a bank
and an accountants' office; the 'skilled non-manual' category included various kinds of office-workers and civil servants; the
'skilled manual' category included an upholsterer, a playgroup
worker, a hairdresser and a hotel worker; the 'semi-skilled' category included a nursing auxiliary and a telephonist, and the
'unskilled' category included various kinds of shop and factory
workers, some farmworkers and a kennel maid. Five parents could
not be categorized in this way as none of them had been in paid
employment outside the home since leaving school: they are
referred to as 'parent' in table 3.2.

We were naturally concerned that those parents who left the
sample might affect its overall socio-economic distribution. There
was in fact a slight tendency for those leaving to come from
unskilled or manual occupations rather than non-manual or professional occupations. However, as the numbers involved were
small, it did not have any major effect on the overall distribution
of the sample.

While we were fairly confident that the parents ranged widely
across the socio-economic spectrum, we could not make the same
claim about their representing a wide range of ethnic groups. In
fact, the sample was typical of this area of England, in that it
contained relatively few members of ethnic minorities. While this
is clearly a limitation of the study, it was not one over which we
had much control, given the resources available to us.

In the course of the interview we also enquired, as tactfully as
we could, about the parent's marital status. At the time of the first
interviews, the great majority of parents (81 per cent) were living
with the child's other parent, 14 per cent were single parents and
4 per cent were living with another partner. Inevitably there were
some changes to the parents' marital status as the study proceeded,
with some parents separating, some re-marrying, and others decid-
ing to live with another partner.

At the time of the first interviews, the children who were the
focus of our study were aged between 5 years 3 months and 6
years 3 months, with a mean age of 5 years 9 months. Quite
unintentionally, there turned out to be exactly the same number

of girls as boys in the sample (69 of each). The average family size was 2.3 children, and nearly half the children (61) had a brother or sister at the same school. As we shall see, the experiences of these other children sometimes had an important influence on how the parents saw the school.

How the interviews were carried out

Almost all the interviews were carried out by two members of the research team (FW and TN), with the remaining few being carried out by the third (MH). We were careful to ensure that each parent was re-interviewed each year by the same interviewer who had interviewed them initially: our impression was that parents expected to see the same interviewer again and would not have been quite so open if a new interviewer had appeared instead. It was also an important part of our methodology that we would remind parents about what they had said on previous occasions: not only would this have been less natural coming from a different interviewer, but it might also have been seen as a breach of confidentiality. We were all parents ourselves, and this may have helped us on occasions to empathize with the parents during an interview.

We were usually received warmly by the parents, and offered tea, coffee or the occasional gin and tonic. The interviews themselves were almost always pleasant and enjoyable, as the parents appreciated the opportunity to talk at length about their children's education. Indeed, the interviews tended to get longer each year, partly because the parents seemed more relaxed and open as they got to know us better, and partly because there was more to talk about as the study proceeded.

The project timetable meant that almost all the interviews were carried out in the autumn and winter. This meant that we frequently found ourselves in unfamiliar areas on dark afternoons or evenings, looking for remote farms down unlit lanes or trying to locate families on inhospitable housing estates. Not surprisingly, there were occasions when we felt quite apprehensive about what might be awaiting us, although these feelings were usually offset by the warm welcome on our arrival.

The interviews contained between 50 and 70 questions each year, grouped into the six main areas outlined in chapter 1. The parents were encouraged to express their views freely and fully: if in the course of answering one question they answered others as well, then these were not asked again. It usually took between 45 and 60 minutes to complete each interview, although it sometimes took longer if a parent became particularly enthusiastic or detailed in their replies.

Each interview was tape-recorded using a small portable tape-recorder. None of the parents objected to this, although occasionally one would ask for the tape-recorder to be switched off when they wanted to make a particularly confidential remark. The interviewers in any case assured the parents of complete confidentiality, and made it clear that nothing they said would be reported back to the school. The study was presented to the parents as being about their views on the changes currently under way in education, and it was explained that the findings would hopefully be of value to practising teachers and those in training. This justification appeared quite acceptable to the parents: indeed, many expressed the opinion that parents' views were not sufficiently taken account of in schools. Some parents used the interview as an opportunity to ask us for information about current reforms, and we had to tread a fine line between maintaining rapport and not providing the answers to subsequent questions.

While we were usually able to get the parents' undivided attention, there were inevitably occasions when we had to compete with the other demands on their lives. Interviews were frequently conducted with a baby or small child sitting on the parent's knee, playing around the interviewer's legs or watching TV in the same room. On one occasion a child watched 'Batman' with the sound turned up so loudly that the interview was virtually inaudible on the tape-recording. Pets also played an unexpectedly large part in the proceedings. Interviews would be cancelled if a pet was ill, cats would occasionally knock the tape-recorder on the floor or steal it altogether, while dogs either showed the interviewer how friendly they were or lurked menacingly in the background – one family had a 15-stone Rottweiler which lived in its own replica house in the back yard, while other dogs were smaller but closer!

Telephone interviews about SATs

While the great bulk of our data came from these annual face-to-face interviews, there was one occasion during the study when we adopted a different technique. During the summer of 1991, all the children in the project took part in the first ever national assessment of 7-year-olds. In the first half of the summer term, the children were assessed using standardized assessment tasks (SATs). This phase of the assessment process provoked a huge amount of media attention, which was quite unforeseen when we planned the study.

In view of this high level of public attention being given to the SATs, we decided to carry out a short telephone interview with our parents immediately after they had taken place. These interviews focused on the parents' knowledge of the SATs and their immediate reaction to them: in addition, the parents were asked to predict what levels their child would reach in the three core subjects of English, maths and science. A few of the parents did not have telephones, were ex-directory, or were simply unobtainable, but we were still able to obtain data from 111 parents by this method. Those parents who could not be reached by telephone were subsequently asked the same questions in our Year 3 interviews later that year. More details of the telephone interviews, and the events leading up to them, can be found in chapter 9.

Did our interviews affect the parents?

One of the problems in conducting any kind of research is that the process of carrying out the research may have some kind of distorting effect on what is being researched. In this case, the danger was that, by repeatedly asking parents detailed questions about current developments in education, we might have been making them unusually sensitive to these developments. This could merely have increased their interest in what was going on, but it could conceivably have resulted in their taking some action – such as confronting the school on a particular issue or moving their child to another school – purely because of our research.

We tried to evaluate this possibility at the end of the final interview. We asked the parents what effect they felt our questions had had on them and on their interaction with the school. The most common response, given by nearly half the parents, was that the interviews had made them think more deeply about the issues involved. At the same time, very few parents felt that being involved in the research had changed the way they had actually behaved. The following comments were typical of many:

> I think it has just made me sit back and think about it, but it hasn't changed anything. I've always had good communication with the school.

> It's made me give more thought to the National Curriculum. Because I know you're coming asking questions I try to take it in more. But it hasn't changed my behaviour.

> It's made me think more about the questions I've never asked at the school. It's made me think more about the work my child's doing.

One parent described his feelings in rather different terms. He was a senior teacher at another school, and felt strongly critical of some aspects of the current reforms. Our interviews provided him with an opportunity to express some of these feelings:

> I feel much better after your interviews. It's like having a confessional or a therapeutic session. It saves me having to write to the Education Minister.

The parents' claims that the interviews had not changed their behaviour were supported by comments made by the headteachers of the 11 schools at the end of the study. The heads said they had received little or no feedback from parents about the research, apart from the occasional comment that they had found it 'interesting' or 'useful'. The heads also claimed that the research had had no effect on the interaction between parents and the school, although one head did say it had made her more aware of the need to keep parents informed.

It seems reasonable to conclude that our research had not had a major effect on the parents' behaviour or on their interaction with the school. At the same time, it seems to have made them more thoughtful and aware of the issues involved. While it could be argued that this casts doubt on the validity of our findings, we prefer to take a more positive view. We believe that the views and opinions expressed by parents in our interviews should be treated with greater respect precisely because they *are* the product of thought and reflection, rather than a glib response produced on the spur of the moment.

The analysis of the interviews

In the course of the project we collected a large amount of data from parents. One of our biggest tasks was to analyse these data in order to make sense of what had been said and to provide answers to our research questions. The approach we adopted was as follows.

For each set of interviews we developed a coding system, based both on what the parents had actually said and (for Years 2 and 3) on how we had coded similar questions previously. The coding system allowed us to make a *quantitative* coding for each question, whereby the parent's response was allocated to one of a small number of categories. Thus the parents' responses to the question 'how far do you see yourself as a consumer of education?' were coded as either 'not at all', 'to some extent' or 'very much so'. In addition, we noted any comments which the parent made which illuminated their response in some way. Sometimes, these comments were similar to those made by other parents, and so they were assigned to particular categories – what we termed a *qualitative* coding. For example, several parents responded to the consumer question along the lines of 'no, I see the child as a consumer', and so the second half of this response was coded as 'child is consumer'. Other responses were unique, such as the parent who commented 'oh, the school as supermarket – no, we're no more conducive to that metaphor than we were last time', and such comments were simply noted as they stood. In order to ensure high levels of inter-coder agreement, every interview was coded by two different researchers and any disagreements were negotiated until agreement was reached.

The system allows us to present our findings in both a quantitative and a qualitative manner. Thus in the example given above, we will present in a table the percentage of parents each year whose responses fell into each of the three main quantitative categories. It should be noted that sometimes questions were not asked, and so the total *n* in some of the tables is less than the full sample size for that year. In addition, the parents' responses were sometimes uncodable, so the percentages given may not always add up to 100 per cent. There were sufficient parents in the sample for us to carry out statistical tests on whether there were any significant changes in these overall percentages from one year to the next. We were able to use the qualitative codings to throw more light on why particular parents responded in the way they did, and why their responses changed (or did not change) from one year to the next. As we have already seen in chapter 2, a similar but less complex system was used for analysing the headteachers' data.

Overview

In this chapter we have described how we actually interviewed the parents. The main points to note are as follows:

- In Year 1, 138 parents were interviewed from 11 contrasting schools in the southwest of England.
- 128 of these parents were re-interviewed in Year 2, and 124 in Year 3.
- It was usually the mother who was interviewed.
- The parents came from a wide range of occupations, but there were few parents from ethnic minorities.
- The parents were interviewed face-to-face in their homes,

although in Year 3 we also carried out telephone interviews about the SATs.

- Few parents felt their behaviour had been affected by the interviews.
- The interviews were analysed using both quantitative and qualitative methods.

4

Parents as Consumers

It's not entirely like buying a packet of biscuits – you're putting in as much as you're taking out.
(Parent's comment on her role as a consumer)

At the heart of the current educational reforms is the idea that parents should be regarded as consumers with respect to their children's education. As we saw in chapter 1, the success or failure of the reforms depends crucially on the extent to which parents will take on this role, and particularly on the extent to which they will make choices between schools on the basis of publicly available information about academic performance. Schools, for their part, are being increasingly urged to treat parents as their customers or clients, and to provide the kind of service which parents appear to want. It is assumed that the introduction of 'market forces' into education in this way will lead inexorably to higher standards in schools.

Quite what is meant by the term 'consumer', and how far it is appropriate to see education in such terms, is a matter of considerable debate. In a recent discussion of these issues Woods (1993) points out that the term 'consumer' is problematic, and that it is 'vigorously contested because of its associations with the principles of the free market and competition' (p. 9). Woods' own approach is not to reject the term out of hand but to develop instead the concept of the 'consumer-citizen'. This concept, he argues, can be applied to a wide range of goods and services which citizens in various ways make use of. The role involves a number of characteristic activities, such as making choices, checking that the service meets the consumer's own needs, carrying out quality assurance, and attempting to influence the decision-making process. Woods argues that the consumer-citizen is characterized by being in 'a relatively disadvantaged position with regard to power in relation to producers and other decision-makers (administrators and politicians)' (p. 19). He also suggests that the concept of the consumer-citizen can be 'utilised as a yardstick with which to study the perceptions and actions of parents' (p. 19).

Woods' comment that the term 'consumer' is problematic would no doubt be shared by many of the headteachers who took part in our telephone survey (see chapter 2). While the majority of these heads told us that they saw their parents as consumers, at least to some extent, this perception was frequently accompanied by some sort of qualification. Many heads said they disliked the term and its connotations, or that they would rather see children as consumers, or that they preferred to think of parents as 'partners'. As we noted earlier, our impression was that many heads were paying little more than lip-service to the notion of parents as consumers: their advantaged position within the educational market meant they had not yet been required to make any major concessions to parental demand.

Our aim in this chapter is to look at the issue of consumerism from the perspective of the parents in our study. We shall address the following questions:

- How far did the parents see themselves as consumers?
- What did they seem to understand by the term?
- Did their views change over the course of the study, and if so, why?
- Did the parents think they were seen as consumers by their children's schools?

Parents' perceptions of themselves as consumers

In the course of the first interview the parents were asked how far they saw themselves as a 'consumer' when thinking about their child's education. Their initial reaction to this question was quite striking. Many parents seemed unfamiliar with the term 'consumer', or at least with its use in this particular context, and almost half of them (45 per cent) found the question puzzling or difficult to answer. Blank looks or puzzled expressions were common, as well as reactions such as 'What do you mean?', 'In what respect?', 'I don't understand the question' and 'I don't think like that'. One parent shook his head and replied 'I'm a farmer, simple as that'.

When researchers find that one of their questions is causing puzzlement or difficulty, they usually replace it with one which is easier to understand. In this case we deliberately did not do so. We found it very revealing that a phrase which was readily used by politicians and educationalists appeared somewhat alien to a large proportion of the people to whom it was supposed to apply. Of course, this does not mean that these parents were not behaving as consumers, or that they were not thinking along consumerist lines. It does imply, however, that many parents might have difficulty in identifying themselves when politicians refer to parents as 'consumers of education', or in appreciating the role they are required to play within the current reforms.

In terms of our research, we had a practical problem in knowing how to continue with the interview if a parent found the question puzzling. We solved this problem by explaining to such parents that the term 'consumer' was a term with which they might be familiar from other contexts, such as shopping or using a public service, and that it was currently being applied to education. We then asked them again how far they saw themselves in this way. Eventually we were able to assign almost all the parents' responses to one of the three categories shown in figure 4.1, although there were still some parents who could not be categorized this way.

As figure 4.1 shows, only a small minority of parents said they saw themselves 'very much' as consumers. These parents seemed to have a clear sense of what it meant to be a consumer, and this fitted closely with how they saw education. One parent, who had used private education before moving into the state system, explicitly compared sending her child to school with making a purchase at a shop:

It's like going out and spending your money on something – are you getting value for money?

Other parents who unequivocally regarded themselves as consumers linked the idea of consumerism with that of choice. One such parent lived in a village which did not have a primary school and had been required to choose from a number of surrounding villages which did have schools:

If I had had only one school to choose from I might not have thought of myself as a consumer, but as I had choice I did.

About half the parents said they did not see themselves 'at all' as consumers (see figure 4.1). While in some cases this may simply have reflected their puzzlement with the term, or their lack of familiarity with it in the educational context, there were still many parents who gave detailed justifications for their answer. These justifications were of two main kinds. First, there were some parents who were strongly opposed in principle to seeing education in consumerist terms. As in the following

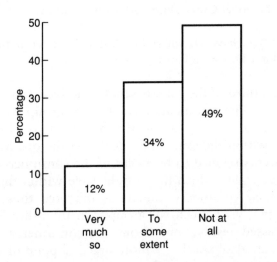

Figure 4.1 How far do parents see themselves as consumers? (Year 1, *n* = 137.)

example, their objections arose from their deeply rooted beliefs about education:

> I hate the whole idea of thinking of education as a commodity. It's hideous. Education is about creating people and personalities.

But there were also several parents who felt that the idea of being a consumer simply did not fit with the reality of using state education in their particular locality. Some of their comments suggested that this was an inevitable consequence of being in the state sector, as opposed to using private education. For example:

> Not in the slightest – you take what you get with the state system.

> If we'd gone private, then maybe, but as we're not buying it's not appropriate.

Other parents mentioned specific features of the state system which precluded their acting as consumers. In particular, they pointed to their inability to influence decisions, or their lack of knowledge of their rights:

> With the National Curriculum parents have no say.

> I suppose you have certain rights, but I don't see it that way. Parents don't know enough to be consumers.

Just over a third of the parents saw themselves 'to some extent' as consumers. The comments made by this group were particularly interesting, as they frequently showed signs of conflicting viewpoints within the same individual. On the one hand, many of these parents seemed to be aware of the consumerist perspective, and the rights which they might have within this perspective: thus their comments sometimes mirrored those made by parents in the 'very much so' group. On the other hand, they often expressed reservations about the consumerist approach, either from an ideological or a more practical point of view: thus their comments frequently reflected those made by parents in the 'not at all' group. The possible conflict or ambivalence between these different points of view is clearly revealed in some of the following comments. The next two parents, for example, combine a growing acceptance of the consumerist perspective with a certain reluctance or regret:

> I will expect to be a consumer more because of the National Curriculum, but I still find it hard to use the term.

> To a certain extent, in that we must keep an eye on what is going on, but I regret the passing of trust between parent and teacher.

Other parents felt that the constraints on their capacity to take on the consumerist role lay within the school. This point is illustrated in different ways by the following two comments. The first parent expressed the limitations more positively (although somewhat confusingly) in terms of teachers' professionalism, while the second saw it more in terms of the power which the teachers held over her child:

> You have to be able to choose how your child is taught – it is *your* child – but teachers know best when it comes to education.

> I feel I have the right to say no but I'm not listened to by the school. Perhaps if I went through the right channels, but at present if I moan and groan it will be a rod for my daughter's back.

There were also parents who did not object outright to the consumerist perspective, but who felt that it had only a limited relevance to education. Again, this point was expressed in different ways:

> Academic services cannot be put on a commercial level – it's a different ethos. But you can choose. You can select and have a say in what your children are taught to a certain extent.

> It's not entirely like buying a packet of biscuits – you're putting in as much as you're taking out.

Asking parents how far they saw themselves as 'consumers' had clearly generated some interesting responses. The parents' initial reaction to the question suggested that many of them found the idea unfamiliar or puzzling. Amongst those who were more at ease with the term, opinions were divided. Some parents felt happy to identify themselves as consumers, while others expressed distaste for the term; others again displayed what can only be termed a reluctant acceptance of being a consumer.

The parents' comments also threw some light on what they understood by the term 'consumer'. For many parents, being a consumer was centrally about choice: there were those who saw themselves as consumers because they had exercised choice, as well as those who did not see themselves this way because they had had little or no choice of school. But the notion of being a consumer also went beyond choice, in that for many parents it was associated with having some sort of knowledge about – and influence over – what was going on in their children's school. Typically, this perspective was put forward by parents who felt constrained in these areas, and who saw these constraints as limitations on their role as consumers.

Changes in parents' perceptions during the study

In Years 2 and 3 the parents were again asked how far they saw themselves as consumers with respect to their children's education. We reminded them on each occasion of how they had replied the previous year, and asked whether they still felt the same.

The difficulty which many parents had initially experienced with the question was not quite so evident in subsequent years. This was possibly because they were becoming more familiar with the notion of being a consumer, or possibly because they were getting more used to being asked about it! But there was still a small group of parents (around 10 per cent each year) who found the question just as difficult when encountering it for the second or third time. These parents typically made comments such as 'I still find it difficult to think like that', or 'I'm still not really sure what you mean'. Some parents had evidently been thinking about the question in the intervening year, while there were others who greeted its reappearance with something approaching familiarity

Table 4.1 Changes in parents' perceptions of themselves as consumers

	Year 1 (n = 137)	Year 2 (n = 128)	Year 3 (n = 124)
Very much so	12%	13%	16%
To some extent	34%	42%	52%
Not at all	49%	40%	29%

or amusement – 'I was wondering when you'd ask me that' or 'that one again!' One parent laughed sardonically and commented:

> Oh, the school as supermarket – no, we're no more conducive to that metaphor than we were last time.

As before, we were eventually able to assign virtually all the parents' responses in Years 2 and 3 to one of the three main categories described earlier. The overall distribution of these responses is shown in table 4.1 with the results from Year 1 shown again for comparison. As can be seen, the parents became increasingly likely to see themselves as consumers over the period of the study. While there was only a small increase in the proportion of parents who considered themselves 'very much' as consumers, there was a much larger (and statistically significant) increase in the number of parents who considered themselves 'to some extent' as consumers, and a comparable decrease in the proportion of parents responding 'not at all'.

In order to understand more about the nature of these changes, we looked more closely at individual parents and how their responses changed over the three years of the study. This analysis was based on 114 parents whose data were available for each of the three years. We found that nearly two-thirds of the parents (66 per cent) did not actually change their perceptions over the period of the study. We also found that virtually all the parents whose views did change moved in the direction of becoming 'more like consumers'. By far the most common change was from saying 'not at all' in Year 1 to saying 'to some extent' in Years 2 or 3.

Why did some parents change their perceptions while others did not? Were the changes due to specific events or experiences which made them re-think their position, or were they a more gradual response to the changing educational climate? We can gain some insights into these questions by looking more closely at the parents' own comments.

Parents whose perceptions did not change

It is usually much harder to elicit an explanation from someone for why their views have *not* changed than for why they have. This is partly because the social conventions of an interview make it harder to probe for reasons in the absence of change. Thus if a parent has just said that there is no change in her views, it is not easy to ask 'why is that?': the question suggests that she should have changed her position, and she is immediately thrown on the defensive. It is not surprising, then, that many of the parents whose views did not change provided little insight into why this might be.

This point is well illustrated by the following parent. She lived on the same estate on which she had grown up, and had little experience of life beyond the estate. Her replies to other questions suggested that, for both her and her unemployed husband, school was essentially something to be endured rather than enjoyed. She was happy to be interviewed, and talked a lot about her children's difficulties and accomplishments. However, she answered many questions as minimally as possible:

Year 1   Not really.
Year 2   Still feel the same.
Year 3   Same.

Other parents, however, provided more extensive comments, despite the absence of change in their views. Several of these parents appeared to hold firm opinions which were relatively unaffected by the passage of time. This point is illustrated in contrasting ways by the next two parents. The first parent had left school at the earliest possible opportunity, but still showed a strong interest in and understanding of educational issues. Her husband came from abroad and had been forced to return home to get work as his qualifications were not recognized in England. This parent strongly rejected the consumerist perspective: her comments each year served to restate her feelings that it was inherently unfair and that the country should invest in education as 'its future':

Year 1
(Not at all)

No, I don't, because I expect education to be a high standard. It's the future of the country. They should put all their resources into it.

Year 2
(Not at all)

If I had money I would want the best for the children but the majority of people in this country are working-class and just get by. Education is the future. It's an investment in this country and shouldn't be neglected.

Year 3
(Not at all)

I don't agree with it. Education should be the same wherever you are. It's different if you're well off and got two cars. Some people can't go to schools a long way off; they have to rely on the closest school.

The following parent was equally consistent in her views, although they were of a different nature. Her husband was a policeman and she worked part-time as a hairdresser. They were both very pleased with the school their daughters attended, but felt it was their responsibility to make sure they got the best education possible. They made it clear they would consider private education if they felt this was not happening:

Year 1
(Very much so)

A lot. We thought about private but it's too expensive. We do look around . . . I think we're getting a good education.

Year 2
(Very much so)

They are our kids. It would only be the expense that would stop us opting for private if we weren't happy with the school and couldn't get into a school we liked. The school is providing

a service and it is up to us to judge its quality.
A pity more parents don't.

Year 3   If we could afford private we would because of
(Very much so) the size of the classes. There's big classes at this
                school, although it's not affecting her at present.

Our overall impression, then, was that many of the parents
whose views did not change were expressing deeply rooted beliefs about education. For these parents, little had happened between interviews to make them question or rethink these beliefs.

Parents who saw themselves more as consumers

Almost all the parents whose responses changed during the course
of the study saw themselves increasingly as consumers. These
parents fell into two main groups. The first group consisted of
those whose views had apparently been changed by some specific
event or experience: these parents explicitly linked their increasing perception of themselves as consumers to particular circumstances in their lives. For the second group of parents, however,
the change in their views was the result of something less con-
crete: these parents seemed to be responding more to the changing educational climate than to any particular experience. We shall
look at each group in turn.

Several parents in the first group explicitly linked their increasing perceptions of themselves as consumers to the issue of secondary choice. Many of the children in the study had an older
brother or sister who had recently transferred to secondary schools,
or was about to do so, and their parents had been involved in the
process of visiting and selecting schools. These experiences had
led some of the parents to think more deeply about their role as
consumers, and although a different child was involved, it had
affected the way they thought about their younger child's education. This point is well illustrated by the following parent, who
is particularly clear-cut in the way he changes his position on

'shopping around'. This father had twin daughters who were approaching secondary transfer but whom he thought had little chance of a place in the local grammar school. Between the Year 2 and Year 3 interviews he and his wife had been out looking at alternatives:

Year 1 (Not at all)	Not really. I'm from the old school. You go to the local school, that's your only choice. I wouldn't shop around for education.
Year 2 (Not at all)	I still feel the same.
Year 3 (To some extent)	With secondary education coming up we are shopping around trying to find the best school. It's hard to get an opinion. It's hard to work out.

In addition to parents who were concerned about secondary transfer for their elder children, there were many parents who were already thinking about this for their younger child (see chapter 5 for further discussion of this point). For several of these parents, their concern over this issue was influencing their perceptions of themselves as consumers. This was particularly pronounced for those parents, like the one above, who lived in areas where the 11-plus and selective secondary education were still operating. The following parent, for example, had just moved into the area from London at the time of the first interview. By the second interview she had got to know the local set-up and was becoming increasingly aware of the lack of real choice at the secondary stage:

Year 1 (Not at all)	I don't really see myself that way.
Year 2 (To some extent)	But I don't feel that we have that much choice. I'm worried about secondary. If they don't go to the grammar school there's no other choice but the local college, and I've not heard good reports about it.

Year 3   But I don't like the question. It's the same with
(To some extent)   the senior schools, there's not a lot of choice.

These comments show how being involved in (or even just contemplating) the transfer of children to secondary school was one of the main factors underlying parents' increasing perceptions of themselves as consumers. But it was not the only factor which appeared to be operating. Some parents suggested that the change in their views had been caused by changes in their relationship with the school. One parent, for example, specifically linked the change in her attitude with her increasing involvement in the school, and in particular with her instrumental role in setting up a PTA (Parent Teacher Association). In the first interview she commented on the fact that she had been unable to get her children into her first choice school. She subsequently started to get more involved as she felt unhappy with the limited information she had been given when she asked about her children's progress. She felt that comments like 'he's fine' were of little value to her:

Year 1   Not so much at the moment. Choices are
(Not at all)   limited. Maybe attitudes will change. . . .

Year 2   Still limited.
(Not at all)

Year 3   Don't know – I suppose, yes. I've become more
(To some extent)   involved. I've asked more. I started the PTA
                       to find out more. Unless you go in you don't
                       know as you're not informed.

Another parent felt that the change in her views was due to a sharp deterioration in her relationship with her child's school. She and her husband both worked full-time and felt they had little contact with the school; however, they bought their son a reading book each week and looked carefully at all the work he brought home from school. Although they had been told by their son's teacher that he was doing fine, he performed poorly in English in the standardized assessments at the end of Year 2. As his mother told us in the final interview, she had been very upset by his

report, which she said 'made him out to look a little thicky'. This
had in turn affected how far she saw herself as a consumer:

Year 1   I don't. Education is there, although I suppose
(Not at all)   we do pay for it.

Year 2   No change.
(Not at all)

Year 3   I would say I was more now since things have
(To some extent) happened. I'm now looking at the possibility
                of a different school.

The second main group of parents were those who increasingly
saw themselves as consumers but who did not put this down to
particular events or circumstances. Rather, the change in their
views seemed due more than anything to the passage of time.
Perhaps the most clear-cut example of this was the only parent
whose responses changed from 'not at all' to 'very much so' during
the course of the study. This parent had not done well at school
herself but was determined to learn alongside her daughters.
During the period of the study she took and passed several GCSEs
at the local comprehensive school. She and her husband had considered private education but could not afford it for all their children; they had therefore decided to try the local school and make
sure it provided the best for their children. The father had become
a governor and the mother was involved both on a daily basis in
the classroom and with the PTA. She told us that the opportunity
to reflect on the matter between interviews had led her to a different opinion:

Year 1   I've not thought about it. I don't really see myself
(Not at all)   in those terms.

Year 2   I feel differently. I've thought about it since you
(Very much so) were last here. We're very much clients. It's up
                to the school to prove their worth for our
                children.

Year 3   Still feel the same.
(Very much so)

It was more common for parents to talk in terms of an increased general awareness, or a sense that 'this is the way things are going'. This awareness seemed to be coming from many different sources, including the school, the media, and other parents. Many of the parents felt somewhat uneasy about these changes, and while they were increasingly seeing themselves as consumers, they did so with varying degrees of hesitancy or reluctance. This point is well illustrated by the parent quoted below. Her own schooling had not progressed beyond the secondary level, and she had strong beliefs about the importance of education. She had decided not to send her daughter to the local school as the child was very shy and her mother felt she needed a smaller school; she had therefore sent her to a small village school some 5 miles away. Despite this clear example of consumer choice the mother said in the first two interviews that she did not consider herself a consumer:

Year 1 (Not at all)	I don't think I ever have. Unless you've got a lot of money . . . it's a national right, or it should be.
Year 2 (Not at all)	I still feel the same. I would only change if I came into money and could choose to go private – but even then I don't think I would bother.
Year 3 (To some extent)	I still feel it's a child's right but the government are turning us into consumers now. For example, if they bring in a league of results I'd be bound to look at them. The Conservatives are turning us into consumers.

Parents who saw themselves less as consumers

There were three parents who went against the dominant trend and saw themselves *less* like consumers as the study proceeded. In view of the unexpected nature of this change, we will examine the views of all three parents in full.

The first parent had a child with severe language problems who attended a special unit for part of the time he was in the project. During this period he progressed well. The child then returned to mainstream education. His mother was not happy with the new arrangements and felt he was not getting the extra support which he needed and which had been promised. The whole process involved a large amount of bureaucracy and left the mother feeling frustrated and helpless. Her comments suggest that it is not so much that her views on consumerism had changed, but rather that her sense of powerlessness had increased as a result of her experiences:

Year 1 (To some extent)	In some ways. You basically accept what is put in front of you. You can't change the school.
Year 2 (Not at all)	I don't feel I can change things, although there's a lot I would like to. There's cutbacks all the time. There's not much that parents can do really.
Year 3 (Not at all)	Still the same.

The second parent in this group worked as a teacher at a local secondary school. Unlike the previous parent, his comments did not draw on his own experiences as a parent, but were at a more abstract level. It is as if the question gave him an opportunity to reflect aloud on the underlying issues and that, over the years, his reflections led him to conclude that he did not after all see himself as a consumer. By the end of the final interview he had completely redefined his position:

Year 1 (To some extent)	I think I am. I make judgements. Parents are seen by politicians as consumers, but it is not a quantifiable thing, there's so many other considerations. You're a consumer in that you have access to governors – although that has both positive and negative aspects.
Year 2 (To some extent)	I feel the same. But it's the wrong model for education. Actually, I don't think as consumers

parents have enough specialist knowledge to
assess what's going on.

Year 3
(Not at all)

I still don't like the industrial model. It's about
relationships, not a conveyor belt with a product. About individuals – about the unknown
as often as not. I don't regard myself as a consumer, I regard the children as consumers.

The third member of this group was also professionally involved in education, as a student-teacher. The change in her
perceptions seemed due to a mixture of conceptual and personal
reasons. Indeed, it is almost as if her definition of 'consumer'
changed over time rather than her perception of how far the term
applied to herself:

Year 1
(To some extent)

I think things seem to have changed. I probably
have more say now – for example, there are
parent governors on the governing body. It's
easier to go in and chat to the headmistress.

Year 2
(To some extent)

I feel that because the head is now taking a
class I can't go in and talk to her, but with
regard to the rest, yes.

Year 3
(Not at all)

I think I would now say that children are the
consumers. I've made the choice, but in regard
to education – they're the consumers. I've come
to realize it's the children that have to go
through the changes, not me.

It is almost certainly no coincidence that these two parents
who were both professionally involved in education should say
that 'the children are the consumers': as we saw in chapter 2, this
comment also occurred frequently in our sample of headteachers.
Indeed, the comments of these last two parents bear a much greater
resemblance to those of the headteachers than they do to the
responses of other parents.

This detailed examination of the comments made by parents
whose views changed – as well as by those whose views did not

change – has given us some insight into what might underlie change. Clearly, the issue is complex: parents differ in a variety of ways, and it is not easy to reduce this complexity to a few simple generalizations. Nevertheless, it would seem that a number of factors are involved. First, this is evidently an issue which touches on many parents' deeply rooted beliefs about the nature and purpose of education. In some cases these beliefs fit closely with the emerging perspective of education as a market, but in other cases they do not. But the parents' comments are not simply reflections of their underlying beliefs: other factors are also operating. One of these is the parent's own experience of inter-acting with the state education system. Having to make choices for an 11-year-old, or feeling a sense of powerlessness or lack of voice within the system, are all experiences which are likely to interact with parents' belief systems and affect whether they see themselves as consumers. The other major factor which is appar-ently operating is a growing realization – however grudging – that times are changing, and that deeply rooted beliefs may not be applicable to the present climate. It is the interplay of all these factors which we are seeing in these parents' responses, and in the way they change over time.

Does the school see you as a consumer?

In the final interview we followed up the question of whether parents saw themselves as consumers by asking if they thought the *school* saw them as a consumer. The parents' responses to this question are shown in figure 4.2.

As the figure shows, many parents were hesitant about answer-ing this question. Nearly a quarter said they didn't know how the school saw them, and about one in seven thought that the school 'possibly' saw them as consumers. Amongst those parents who did venture an opinion, the numbers who replied 'yes' and 'no' were divided roughly equally.

The comments which the parents made to justify their responses were more revealing, and provide some further insights into what they understood by the term 'consumer'. Several comments

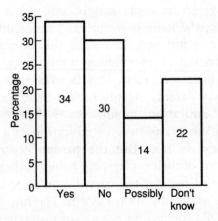

Figure 4.2 Do parents think the school sees them as consumers? (Year 3, $n = 123$.)

indicated that the parents were very aware of the new financial situation in which schools found themselves, and that pupil numbers were of critical importance to the school's finances. The following two parents, for example, justified their response that the school saw them as consumers by referring to the school's need to maintain pupil numbers:

> The head has often commented that he's keen to keep the numbers up. It helps the money coming in.

> Much more so now. They're always worrying about budgets and stuff. I've got a friend who kept her child out of school for a holiday in France, and she was told it didn't do the register any good.

In contrast, the next two parents replied that the school did not see them as consumers. Both parents had children at schools which were relatively secure in their market position, although for different reasons:

> Not really, there isn't any choice. You can't get in anywhere else.

> They're fighting to get in there, so I don't think it makes any difference.

A number of parents did not answer the question simply in terms of the school's position in the local educational market. Rather, they went beyond market issues and talked in terms of their overall relationship with the school. In some cases, the parents talked positively about this relationship, and used it as evidence that the school did regard them as consumers:

> They've always had a good relationship with parents. Always been aware of our needs.

> They do try to inform us, communicate.

Other parents were less happy about their relationship, and as a result queried the extent to which the school saw them as consumers:

> I know they've got to be responsible and attract a certain number of children. But once the children are there I don't know that they do. Do they take account of what parents are saying? I think they rather concentrate on getting children in.

> They're being told to see us as consumers, but it doesn't carry any weight. It depends on how involved you get.

There were limits, however, to the amount of involvement which a school might regard as acceptable. This point was graphically made by the following parent, who referred to her own role as someone who asked awkward questions and generally made life difficult for the school:

> I think they see me as an interfering old bat, actually!

Overview

In this chapter we have looked at how far the parents saw themselves as 'consumers of education'. We have seen that many parents were initially puzzled by the term, although they gradually became more familiar with it over the course of the study. We have also reported a significant increase during the study in the number of parents who regarded themselves as consumers, to some extent at least, and we have indicated some possible reasons for this increase. Finally, we have looked briefly at whether the parents thought they were seen as consumers by their children's schools.

The parents' comments throughout this chapter have provided some insight into their understanding of what it might mean to be a 'consumer of education'. For a large number of parents, being a consumer is centrally about *choice*. Many of those who unequivocally saw themselves as consumers were very aware of having made a choice, while several of those who increasingly saw themselves as consumers had clearly been influenced by having to choose secondary schools for older children, or by their increasing awareness that this was on the horizon for their younger child. In parallel to this, parents who felt constrained or limited in their ability to choose had more reservations about seeing themselves as consumers. The parent who said 'you take what you get with the state system' spoke for many of these parents.

At the same time, many parents made clear that being a consumer is not just about choice: it is also about the continuing *relationship* between parents and schools once the initial choice has been made. Specific elements in the relationship which parents indicated as being important included their knowledge of what is going on in the school, their ability to keep a watching brief over the quality of their child's education, their feeling of being listened to by schools, and their capacity to have a say in the school's decision-making process. If some or all of these elements were present or encouraged by the school, then parents were more likely to see themselves as consumers. Conversely, if they felt constrained or inhibited in any of these areas, then they were less likely to see themselves as consumers. It is interesting that this extended notion of what it means to be a consumer has many similarities with the concept of the 'consumer-citizen' put forward by Woods (1993). Indeed, Woods' argument that consumers are characterized by a relative powerlessness in relation to producers and decision-makers resonates strongly with several of the comments made by parents here.

One final theme which recurred across many of the parents'

responses, and which they shared with the headteachers in our telephone survey, was a strong feeling of *reluctance* or *disquiet* about the whole idea of applying the terminology of the market place to education. While such feelings were not universal, they were expressed by a substantial proportion of both parents and heads, irrespective of how they answered the original question. Comments such as 'I don't like the word consumer' or 'I don't like to think in those terms' recurred again and again in both sets of interviews, and were frequently supported by appeals to alternative ways of talking about education. We were left in no doubt that a large number of the parents and heads whom we had interviewed had serious misgivings about this particular aspect of the current educational reforms.

5

Parents' Choice of School

> Visiting schools felt a bit like invading their territory. It was
> awkward at the end of the visit when you didn't sign up.
>
> *(Parent's comment on choosing schools)*

The central importance of parental choice has been one of the most consistent features of educational policy in England and Wales for the past decade and more. From 1980 onwards a series of Education Acts has attempted to increase parents' ability to choose the school they want their child to attend, and has sought to make schools more responsive to parents' wishes. This policy was continued in the 1988 Education Reform Act, the centre-piece of the current reforms, and has been re-affirmed by the clear statement in the 1992 Education White Paper that 'the Government is firmly wedded to parental choice'. The policy of enhanced parental choice has also been strongly advocated in the United States by both Presidents Bush and Reagan, where the latter has been quoted as saying 'choice works, and it works with a vengeance' (Edwards and Whitty, 1992).

The idea behind increased parental choice is extremely simple. Parents are to be free to choose the school they want their children to attend, while the funding of schools is linked directly to the number of pupils enrolled. Schools which are successful in attracting parents' custom will expand, while those which are not successful will contract and may even be forced to close. Schools will therefore have to raise their standards, and make public the fact they have done so, or they will face extinction. The introduction of market forces in this way, according to the theory, will lead directly to higher standards in education.

While the argument for increased parental choice may be attractive in theory, it has been questioned whether it will necessarily have beneficial effects in practice. One argument against parental choice is that it may result in the inefficient use of resources: popular schools may become overcrowded, while unpopular schools may have large amounts of unused space and equipment. A second argument is that increased parental choice may result in the return of 'selection through the back door': popular schools will be able to choose their parents, rather than parents choosing popular schools. We have in fact already seen evidence of this happening amongst the primary schools surveyed in chapter 2. A third argument is that parental choice may be incompatible with other socially valued ends, such as promoting racial or religious harmony, if parents choose not to send their children to ethnically mixed schools: indeed, a Government Minister, Lady Hooper, has been quoted as saying that 'if parental choice leads to racially segregated schools, then so be it' (Corrigan, 1988; see David (1993), Edwards and Whitty (1992), Johnson (1990) and Miliband (1991) for further discussion of these issues).

A different kind of criticism is that increased parental choice may not work in practice because parents do not actually behave in the way the theory prescribes. In reality, parents may have a very limited degree of choice, or they may choose to send their child to the local school, or they may use criteria other than purely academic performance in choosing schools. There is evidence from research on parental choice carried out before the 1988 Education Reform Act that parents often place more emphasis on factors such as their child's happiness, the child's own wishes, the school's location or the school's reputation for discipline than on factors such as academic performance or examination results (see reviews by Johnson, 1990; David, 1993). While almost all this research has been concerned with parents' choice of secondary school, it is likely that parents behave in a similar way when choosing primary schools. Indeed, one of the few studies of parental choice at this age level concluded that parents were predominantly concerned with issues such as proximity, safety and their child's happiness rather than 'educational content or method' (Petch, 1986).

Our aim in this chapter is to illuminate these issues by looking at how the parents in our study made their choice of school. We had the following questions in mind:

- What reasons did the parents give for choosing schools? Did they choose purely on academic performance, or for other reasons?
- How much choice did the parents exercise in coming to their decision? Did they consider a range of schools, or only one?
- On what basis did the parents make their decisions? Did they actually visit schools, or did they rely on hearsay?
- When do parents start thinking about choice of secondary school? Are their criteria the same as for primary schools?

The complexities of parental choice

At the start of the first interview the parents were asked why they had chosen their child's school, whether they had visited the school before making their choice, and whether they had considered or visited any other school. They were also asked if they had thought about what might happen when their child had to change schools at the age of 11 years. In subsequent interviews they were not asked again about their initial choice of school unless they had actually moved their children to a new school since the previous interview (the small number of parents who did this will be discussed in more detail in chapter 6). However, they were asked again in the final interview about choice of secondary school.

When we came to analyse the parents' responses to these questions, we found the task much more difficult than we had expected. The problem was not so much that our questions were inadequate or inappropriate (although on reflection they might have been expanded) but that the whole issue of parental choice was more complex than we had anticipated. This can be illustrated in a number of ways.

One source of complexity arose because our questions assumed that the parents had chosen the school specifically for the child we were following as part of our study. While this assumption was evidently correct for the great majority of parents, there were some who had actually chosen the school for an older brother or sister – sometimes as much as several years previously. As the school might have changed considerably since the original choice was made, it was by no means clear that the criteria adopted for choosing the school in the first place still applied. Indeed, the fact that an older brother or sister (and in some cases more than one) was already at the school was itself a possible reason for choosing that particular school.

Another source of complexity arose from the notion of 'the local school'. As we shall see, 'locality' was an extremely important factor in the parents' choice of school; however, parents did not necessarily mean the same thing by the term 'local school'. While for some parents this was simply the nearest school, for others it meant the school which parents living in that neighbourhood tended to use, and this was not always the same thing. For example, there were occasions when parents would talk at length about the 'local school' but would completely fail to mention another school which was actually nearer.

A third complicating factor was the issue of private education. For the great majority of parents this was not an issue: either there were no private schools for 5-year-olds in their area, or if there were they could not afford to use them, or if they could afford to use them they refused to do so on principle. At the same time, there were clearly some parents for whom private education was a genuine possibility. However, as we had limited information about the existence of private schools, and even less information about parents' financial liquidity, we decided to ignore the possibility of private education in our analysis of choice. Thus when we talk about parents 'having no choice', we mean that there was no other state school which their child could attend.

Despite these complexities, we were still able to analyse the parents' replies according to two main dimensions. We look first at the reasons parents gave for their choice of school, and then at the degree of choice which they exercised.

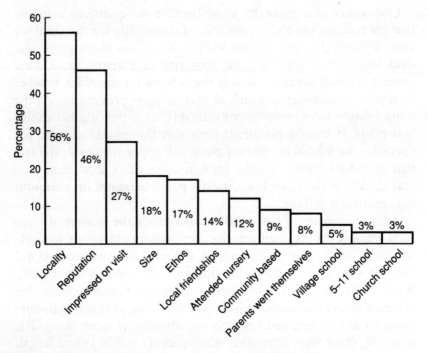

Figure 5.1   Why did parents choose their child's school? (Year 1, *n* = 138.)

Parents' reasons for choosing schools

The principal reasons given by the parents for choosing their child's schools are shown in figure 5.1. Parents frequently gave more than one reason, and so the percentages add up to more than 100 per cent.

The most frequently cited reason for choosing a school was its 'locality'. This suggests that many parents were simply making a choice of convenience, picking the nearest school irrespective of whether or not it was a good school. In fact, there were very few parents who seemed to have chosen the local school purely for its proximity to their home. The great majority of parents who mentioned 'locality' gave additional reasons why they had chosen the local school, in addition to its convenience. Many of these parents emphasized that the school was part of a local community, or that the child's friends would be there, or that it was the village school. Some parents even said that it would have been awkward, if not unthinkable, if they had chosen to send their child to a school which was not the local school:

> We chose the school because we live in the village. Otherwise we would have had to 'opt out'. Not to send your child to the local school could have been seen as being disloyal to your home community.

The second most frequently mentioned reason was the school's 'reputation', or that the school had been recommended by friends or relations. Some parents were not very explicit about why a school had been recommended or exactly what it had acquired a reputation for, simply saying that 'it has a good reputation' or that 'parents are very keen to get their children in there'. Other parents, however, were more specific as to why a school had acquired a certain reputation. Among the most frequently mentioned recommendations were that the teachers were friendly, caring and gave the children plenty of attention:

> I had her down for three schools. This one was recommended by a friend as it was very close in style to her nursery school – small, friendly, and they had time for them.

> My niece went there and she got a good education. They have time to spend one-to-one with the children.

For some parents the reputation of the school was a long-lived thing and did not necessarily bear any reference to recent experience. This was particularly noticeable for those parents who had chosen the school for an older child some years previously. One such parent had two sons three years apart. She had chosen the local school for her elder son as it had a good reputation at the time, and her younger son had automatically followed three years later. Another parent was operating on a much longer time-span. She had two grown-up children who were now teachers themselves: nevertheless, she had still chosen the school they attended for her youngest child because the older children had been happy there, and she felt it had given them 'a good educational start'. For other parents the reputation of the school went back even further still, and was based on their memories of when they themselves attended the school. One parent described how he had moved back into the neighbourhood from another part of the city just before his elder son started school. Although he knew that another school within the area had a better reputation, he chose the nearer one because he had heard there had been few changes since he went there himself as a child.

What is noticeably absent from the list of reasons given by the parents is any major emphasis on academic results, standards or teaching methods. Rather, the parents appeared to place much more importance on social and emotional factors. In particular, what the parents seem to be emphasizing is the importance of continuity and caring: that there should be links with their children's friends, family and community, and that the school should be a welcoming place where their children are valued. This conclusion, it will be noted, fits closely with other research on parental choice reviewed earlier in the chapter: at the same time, it does not fit easily with the notion of parental choice as the main driving force behind the current reforms.

The degree of choice parents exercised

The second dimension along which we categorized parents' choice of schools was the degree of choice which they had exercised. There were three main categories.

> *Category A* contained parents who felt they had had no opportunity to exercise choice at all, as there had only been one school they could choose from.
>
> *Category B* consisted of parents who had had some degree of choice, but who had not exercised it: these parents had only considered one school, although there were other schools from which they could have chosen.
>
> *Category C* was made up of parents who had exercised some

degree of choice: these parents had been able to consider and choose between more than one school.

The number of parents in each category is shown in table 5.1. This table also shows, for each category, whether the parents had chosen the local school (by which we meant the one which was geographically nearest) or whether they had chosen a non-local school.

Table 5.1 The degree of choice parents exercised (Year 1, $n = 138$)

	Chose local school	Chose non-local school	All
A Had no choice	12%	4%	16%
B Only considered one school	34%	4%	38%
C Considered more than one school	21%	25%	46%
Total	67%	33%	100%

Category A: Parents who had no choice

About one in six of the parents (16 per cent) appeared to have had no choice of school (see table 5.1). Most of these parents explicitly described themselves as having no choice, while the others gave accounts which were so similar that we could infer that they too had had no choice. All these parents felt that their choice of school had been determined by factors outside their control, and most of them ended up using the local school.

The parents in this category gave three main reasons for their lack of choice. The most common reason was that other schools were full and could not take their children. In some areas it appeared that several schools were full; here the parents' task was not so much one of choosing a school, but finding one which would have them.

One family, for example, lived on a run-down estate in the

centre of a large city. They had recently moved into this area from another part of the city. The parents soon discovered that although there were three schools in the area which they could in principle use, two of these schools were already full. The parents had reservations about sending their children to the third school as it seemed less secure than the school they had previously attended: it had a large playground with widely spaced railings and was next to a busy road. However, it was their only option.

Another couple had moved from London to a small town prior to the beginning of the school year. When house-hunting from a distance they had located a school which fulfilled their criteria of being a church school and similar to the one their children had attended in London. However, when they arrived in the locality they found that this school was full and could not take their children. They were forced to send their children to another school, further away.

The second main reason why parents felt they had no choice of school was lack of transport. Not surprisingly, this was mentioned most frequently by parents living in rural areas, where the next school was often some distance away. One such family lived on the outskirts of a village. There was a primary school in the middle of the village, while the next school was in the nearest town about 3 or 4 miles away. The mother did not drive, and public transport was so infrequent that it was impossible to take and fetch her daughter from anywhere other than the village school.

Although some children living in rural areas were able to travel on the school bus, their choice of school was frequently determined by the Local Education Authority transport policy which specified the particular school which the children would be bussed to. One parent whose choice was limited in this way was a farmer who shared the farm with his own parents. He lived with his wife and son in a cottage at the bottom of the farmyard, while his parents lived in the farmhouse at the top. The farm was in a small hamlet a few miles from the village which contained the school. The farmer had lived there all his life and had attended the same school as his son. The school bus collected the child each morning from outside the farm gate and took him to the village school. No other choice of school was possible.

The third reason given for lack of choice was of a slightly

different nature. Some parents did not seem to regard sending their children to school as being a matter in which choice played any part. They saw schools in terms of serving a specified catchment area, and assumed that as there was a local school that was where their children had to go. One parent had been led to this belief by the local Education Office. She lived in a large seaside town in which schools had originally been built to serve specific residential areas as they were developed. There were two schools which were roughly equidistant from her home: however, she had understood from the Education Office that only one of the schools was an option for her children.

Category B: Parents who only considered one school

Over a third of the parents (38 per cent) were in category B – that is, they did not consider or visit any other school apart from the one they had chosen for their child, although there appeared to be alternatives available to them. These parents differed from those in category A in that they themselves were responsible for the restrictions on their choice, rather than external circumstances. As table 5.1 shows, almost all the parents in this category sent their children to the local school; the remainder sent their children to the next nearest school.

One family in this category lived on the outskirts of a village which because of development was now very close to the edge of a small town. There were several schools in the town which children living in the village could attend. This family, however, chose the village school without considering any of the schools in town. They did so because they lived in the village, and felt part of that community. The mother also said that she would have chosen a village school anyway, because of her own experiences. She liked the small numbers at the village school.

Another parent lived on the other side of the same village. She also chose the village school without considering alternatives. Her main reason was that it was the local school, but also because it had a good reputation – she pointed out that other parents were very keen to get their children into the school.

Two other parents in this category lived in a large town where there were several different schools to choose from: however, neither parent had considered alternatives to the one they had chosen. One parent chose the school because it was the local school and because of its reputation, but added that she had friends whose children went there. The other parent sent her daughter to the same school for similar reasons. Her next door neighbour's child attended the school and had given her good reports of it. It was not the nearest school to where they lived but was fairly close.

We did not press the parents in this category as to why they had not considered other schools. However, some of the parents gave the impression from their replies that they had just 'struck lucky' first time. That is, they had considered a particular school first, felt it would provide what they wanted and so enrolled their children. Although they did not say so explicitly, they gave the impression that if they had not felt the school would provide what they wanted they would have looked elsewhere.

This category also included several parents who had chosen their house on the basis of which school's catchment area it came within. However, none of these parents had actually looked at more than one school in coming to their decision. One parent was setting up a business in a small town and so wanted to live in the area. As he and his wife had three children they let the location of a suitable school determine exactly where they bought a house. The first school they looked at was in a nearby village. They liked the village, the ethos of the village school and the fact that their children were made to feel welcome, and so bought a house there. Another parent was a young ex-teacher whose husband was a rising executive. They had two children, one of whom was still a baby at the beginning of our study. When they moved into the town they got a list of schools from the Education Office. The first school they looked at had been recommended by some friends who were teachers. They liked the head and the atmosphere, and so they decided to buy a house within the catchment area of the school. A third parent described how she had looked at the schools and the community as a package when moving into the area:

> There is only one school in the village. I looked around first and was quite impressed. When we finalized the sale we got her in. It

is good to stay at school in the village. It's a community-type school.

Category C: Parents who considered more than one school

The third and largest category of parents were those who had considered at least one other school before making their choice. Unlike parents in categories A and B, these parents could be said to have made a genuine choice between two or more alternative schools. As table 5.1 shows, the parents in this category were divided roughly equally between those who chose their local school and those who did not.

Those parents who chose their local school after considering others rarely seemed to have made their choice purely on the basis of convenience. Instead, they were more likely to emphasize the schools' central role in the local community. One parent, for example, lived in a village which had its own primary school. She had considered another school in a nearby town, but decided she wanted her child to have local friends and be involved in the community. Another parent who lived in a city felt it was basically a choice between the local school or another one nearer the city centre. She became involved in the local church and in the playgroup at the local school, and this, together with good reports she had heard of the local school, finally determined her decision.

Other parents who chose the local school after considering others had been influenced by a recommendation or by the school's reputation. One couple felt they were making a choice between the two nearest schools, but said that the one chosen had been recommended by friends. The friends told them it was a warm, caring school with a positive attitude to serving a multi-ethnic community, and that had swayed their decision.

While almost all the parents in this group had made a positive choice of the local school, there were one or two parents whose choice had been determined more negatively. One of these parents was living in a new housing development just off the centre of a small market town. She had moved to the area within the previous year and had started her child at another town centre school. The child had been very unhappy and the parents had not liked the school at all, so after 6 weeks they decided to move him. They tried to get him into another town centre school, as they had heard good reports of it, but it was full. The local school had been the only school that could take him.

Over half the parents in category C had chosen a non-local school after considering others. Many of these parents made this choice because they were not happy with their local school. Sometimes they were not very specific about what they did not like about the local school:

> Because (the one chosen) is the best school around here. The local school I wouldn't give the time of day for.

Other parents were more specific as to why they were 'opting out' of their local school. One parent, who lived in a small village on the west side of a small town, chose to send her sons to another village on the north side of the town as she felt the local school was too big. Her sons were quite shy and she felt they would be lost in a big school. She also wanted a church school and felt it would suit her children better. Another parent lived in a small village which did not have its own school. Children from that village generally went to school in another village nearby, but this parent decided against it as 'we didn't like the atmosphere'. They really wanted their child to attend a second school but it was full. They eventually chose a third school.

Several parents were forced into considering other schools because their first choice was full. One family had had to start looking for another school on the first day of term, as the father explained:

> When we moved here we were told there was no catchment area for School A and they could go there. But when we turned up on the first day we were told there was no room, so we had to start looking around. School B was too far away, and School C was not good for high flyers, but School D (the one finally chosen) is OK.

This detailed analysis of the degree of choice exercised by the parents in our study has revealed something of the complexities of how choices are actually made. It also shows that the meaning of the term 'parental choice' can itself vary according to the particular circumstances in which parents find themselves. On the one hand, there were parents in category A who had no alternative but to send their children to one particular school (usually the local school); for these parents, it is fairly meaningless to talk in terms of 'choosing a school'. On the other hand, there were parents in category C who were able to consider at least one other school, even if this choice was sometimes forced on them, or if their first choice was full. Somewhere in the middle were the parents in category B, who only considered one school: it is not at all clear how far these parents can be said to have exercised 'choice' in coming to their decision. Indeed, it could well be argued that for parents in category B, increased parental choice would be an irrelevancy: they would still behave the same however many schools they could theoretically 'choose' from.

Parents visiting schools

If parents are to play the role of consumer to its fullest extent, making considered choices from a range of schools, then they need appropriate information on which to base their decisions. As we have already seen, many parents in our study appeared to place a good deal of weight on the recommendations of friends and relations. While such recommendations may be extremely valuable, they are by their very nature second-hand: they are not based on the parents' own experiences or observations. An alternative way of obtaining information is to visit schools, and see at first hand what is on offer.

Over half the parents (55 per cent) said they had visited the school before making their choice. However, the proportion of parents visiting varied according to which category they were in. Around 40 per cent of the parents in categories A and B said they had visited the schools, compared with 68 per cent of parents in category C. In other words, parents who had considered more than one school in coming to their decision were more likely to have visited schools as part of the decision-making process.

Some qualifications should be made at this point. First, it was not clear that all parents interpreted the phrase 'visiting the school' in the same way. Some parents seemed to regard a brief chat with the headteacher or secretary as they collected application forms as a 'visit', while others were thinking more in terms of a full-blown tour of the school. In addition, some parents mentioned that they had visited the school *after* their child had been accepted, as part of the school's induction process. While we did not count this as 'visiting the school', it is possible that many parents saw such visits as part of the decision-making process, in that they would have re-thought their decision if they had not liked what they saw at this stage. This point was explicitly made by one parent:

> I visited the school before she started, but not before it was chosen. We plumped for a smaller school. My employers' children went there and they were happy with it. The teacher made a home visit – I liked that. I would have re-considered if I hadn't liked it on the visit. They seemed to take an interest in each child.

Those parents who did not visit the school gave various reasons as to why they had not done so. Some parents said that it was impossible to learn much from visiting a school, so it wasn't worth the effort. Other parents were moving into the area and were limited in the time they could spend looking at schools: in some cases it was more a question of finding a school that would take their children than finding one they liked. Some parents said they did not visit the school as they already knew it well from other contexts. Some parents already had older children at the school and visited it twice a day, while others were regular visitors in that they collected the children of friends or relations, or their child attended a nursery or playgroup based at the school. One mother was a playgroup supervisor and regularly visited the school in this capacity, while another parent remarked:

> I worked as a dinner lady at the school for two years. I thoroughly enjoyed it. I learnt such a lot about the school, and about the children. Every parent should do it!

As we saw in chapter 2, several headteachers in our telephone survey reported that they were increasingly encountering parents who visited a number of schools before coming to their decision. In fact, there was only one parent in our sample who had carried out an extensive programme of visits before making her choice. This mother, a social worker, gave us a detailed account of the various schools she had visited when looking for a suitable school for her eldest child:

> School A had good facilities but seemed very conformist. All the children seemed to be doing the same thing at the same time. It seemed totally geared to middle-ability children. School B had very impressive displays but I had reservations about the head and I didn't like the school ethos. I considered School C but didn't visit it as it wasn't a 5–11 school. At School D (the one finally chosen), all the children were busy, they weren't sitting waiting. The children were doing interesting projects – like on Marilyn Monroe and James Dean. It seemed innovative. It also had a good racial mix – most kids don't see a black face in this part of the world.

This parent's final comment on visiting schools may go some way to explaining why it is not a universal practice:

> Visiting schools felt a bit like invading their territory. It was awkward at the end of the visit when you didn't sign up.

Parents' choice of secondary school

Although our main interest was in how the parents had come to choose the school which their child was currently attending, we asked them in Years 1 and 3 whether they were already thinking about the next major choice they would face, when their child transferred to secondary school. We also asked them how much they would be influenced by published 'league tables' of academic results when they came to make their decision.

We were somewhat surprised to find that the vast majority of parents (84 per cent in Year 1 and 87 per cent in Year 3) had already given serious consideration to what secondary school their child might attend. Even when their child was only 5 years old, most of the parents already knew what the main options were and

were starting to express their preferences. The following comments give some idea of what they had in mind:

> I'm looking for continuity with what she's already getting – an
> awareness of environmental and political issues. I want a school
> that will promote character as well as academic achievement.

> I'd hate to send him to a comprehensive. In my day they were the
> pits. If you weren't clever you went to a comprehensive. I can't get
> that out of my mind. They're so big – like a small town. There
> can't be proper discipline.

> I'm looking for mixed ethnic grouping.

> We want a school with links with farming.

As with their choice of primary school, many parents said that
their choice of secondary school was either limited or non-existent.
The issue was complicated in some areas by the continued presence
of the 11-plus system, and the effect this had on choice. There
were other limitations on choice too:

> Choice is restricted by lack of transport. They need a safe journey
> to and from school.

> I'm horrified by the lack of choice. It's basically a choice between
> the not too bad and the dreadful.

Just under half the parents thought their choice of secondary
school would be influenced by published 'league tables', with a
further quarter thinking they might be influenced under some
circumstances. At the same time, most of these parents made clear
that league tables were not the only thing they would consider,
and that other factors were just as important, if not more so:

> I wouldn't just go by results. I'd back it up with my own obser-
> vations, what you hear about them.

> I'd be influenced, but not just by that. I'd go by what the school
> had to offer, which school I feel they'd be happiest at.

Indeed, the overriding impression the parents gave was that choosing a secondary school was not simply a matter of looking up a school's position in a league table, but a much more personal business of matching what was available to the individual needs of a particular child.

Overview

In this chapter we have looked in detail at how the parents in our study chose their children's schools. We have examined the reasons which they gave for choosing the school, the degree of choice which was available to them, the extent to which they visited schools before making their choice, and whether they had started thinking about their child's transfer to secondary school. Three main conclusions can be drawn from their replies.

First, there is little doubt that choice of school is an extremely important issue for parents. It was almost impossible to find a parent who claimed to be indifferent to which school their child went to, even when there was no realistic alternative available to them. It mattered a great deal to the parents that their children went to a school which they felt happy with, and which seemed suited to their child's particular needs. The importance of choice of school was also reinforced by the unexpectedly high proportion of parents who were already thinking about choice of secondary school, even when their children were still in the first years of primary school.

But although choice of school is important to parents, this does not mean that all parents necessarily want the same thing from schools. Nor does it mean that parents will choose schools purely on the basis of their academic performance – a fundamental assumption of the current reforms. In fact, the parents in our study appeared to place much more emphasis on social and emotional factors than on academic ones. Moreover, while this was particularly evident at the start of primary school, there was little sign that parents would be using radically different criteria when they came to choose their children's secondary school: although many parents said they would be influenced by academic 'league tables' at this stage, they made it clear that other factors were just as important. This conclusion fits closely with research on parental choice carried out before the 1988 Education Reform Act and reviewed at the start of the chapter. At the same time, it does not fit easily with the assumption behind the current reforms that parental choice will be the main driving force in raising academic standards.

Our analysis of the degree of choice which parents had actually exercised also raises serious doubts about how parental choice might work in practice. It is assumed by advocates of parental choice that parents will make considered choices from a range of schools, comparing them on the basis of publicly available information, supplemented where possible by first-hand visits. In fact, relatively few parents in our study seemed to behave in such a way. Certainly such a description could not be applied to those parents in category A, who had no realistic alternative to the current school and for whom it is meaningless to talk in terms of 'choice'. Nor is such a description appropriate for those parents in category B, who limited their considerations to a single school. There must even be doubts as to how many parents in category C, who were able to choose between alternative schools, actually carried out detailed comparisons across a wide range of criteria. In other words, there appears to be a serious mismatch between the way in which parental choice is supposed to operate in theory and the way in which parents choose schools in practice.

6

Parents' Satisfaction with Schools

We're very happy with the school. The teachers and head are very supportive. Brilliant!
(Parent's comment on her child's school)

The current educational reforms appear to be based on the assumption of widespread parental dissatisfaction with their children's schools – and particularly with the academic standards which prevail in those schools. The logic behind this assumption is simple: if parents were satisfied with what is currently provided in schools, then what would be the need for reform? But while the argument is superficially attractive, the logic is flawed. The fact that politicians are making major changes to the education system does not necessarily mean that parents are dissatisfied with the way things are at present. It is perfectly possible that parents are generally satisfied with their children's schools, but that their views have been misread, or simply ignored, by the proponents of the current reforms.

In practice, those who are advocating or implementing the current changes tend not to talk explicitly in terms of parental dissatisfaction. Rather, they are more likely to claim that parents 'want higher standards'. As we saw in chapter 1, this argument was used by Kenneth Baker in the House of Commons in 1987, when he proposed that the Education Reform Act would '. . . free schools and colleges to deliver the standards which parents and employers want'. In the same vein, a Department of Education and Science leaflet for parents entitled 'How is Your Child Doing at School?' started with the assertion that 'We all want our children to achieve higher standards' (Department of Education and Science, 1992, p. 2). A similar argument was made by Baroness Blatch, Minister of State for Education, in response to criticisms of the National Curriculum made by Paul Black in 1992:

> Pupils and their parents are entitled to higher standards now, not at some indefinite time in the future. They will certainly not thank us for delaying the reforms unnecessarily just to allow academics more time for debate. (*Times Educational Supplement*, 28 August 1992)

The unstated assumption behind all such claims that parents want higher standards is that they must be unhappy with the standards which currently prevail in their children's schools. Yet there is little evidence from research carried out before the National Curriculum was introduced that parents were dissatisfied with their children's schools. For example, a survey commissioned in 1989 by the Department of Education and Science found that 94 per cent of parents were either 'very satisfied' or 'fairly satisfied' with their child's school (Public Attitude Surveys, 1989). In addition, parents have been reported to be generally satisfied with their child's school in studies of infant schools (Tizard et al., 1988), junior schools (Mortimore et al., 1988) and secondary schools (West, Davies and Scott, 1992). At the same time, there is evidence from public opinion polls that parents do indeed have concerns about 'standards' in state education more generally. For example, a survey carried out in 1990 by Audience Selection for the *Sunday Mirror* found that just over half the parents polled thought that standards were worse now than when they were at school 20 years ago, while a similar proportion thought that children did 'not receive enough education in the 3Rs' (*Sunday Mirror*, 2 September 1990). In other words, parents may be satisfied with their own child's school, but still feel that things are unsatisfactory elsewhere.

This perception of parents was certainly shared by many of the headteachers in our telephone survey. As we saw in chapter 2, these headteachers were virtually unanimous in saying that their parents were either 'satisfied' or 'very satisfied' with their children's school. At the same time, just over a quarter of the heads thought their parents had wider concerns about 'standards' in state education. Many heads, however, felt that these concerns had not arisen directly from the parents' own experiences or observations, but rather had been induced by misleading reports in the media.

In this chapter, we will look at what the parents in our study have to say about these issues. We will address the following questions:

- What did the parents think 'makes a good school'?
- Were the parents happy with their child's school?
- Did they think the teachers were doing a good job?
- Were the parents happy with their child's progress in the 3Rs?
- Were any parents sufficiently unhappy that they moved their child to another school?
- Did the parents have wider concerns about 'standards' in state education?

What do parents think makes a good school?

In the course of the first interview the parents were asked what they thought 'makes a good school'. This was intended as a question about schools in general, and was treated as such by the vast majority of parents: however, there were some parents who answered primarily in terms of their own child's school – what they liked about it and what they felt it was lacking. The parents' responses were repeated back to them during the final interview, and they were asked if they still felt the same. Their responses on each occasion were categorized into a number of distinct factors, such as 'relationships', 'the staff' or 'the atmosphere', and the percentage of parents mentioning each factor is shown in table 6.1. Because many parents mentioned more than one factor, the percentages in each column add up to considerably more than 100 per cent.

Table 6.1 shows the undoubted importance the parents attached

Table 6.1   What do parents think makes a good school?

	Year 1 (n = 137)	Year 3 (n = 124)
Relationships	51%	52%
The staff	46%	41%
The atmosphere	38%	44%
The ethos	38%	34%
Good discipline	27%	28%
Wide-ranging education	19%	18%
The headteacher	16%	15%
Developing the whole child	12%	14%
Academic results	12%	16%
Good resources	8%	9%
Good facilities	7%	6%
Modern methods	6%	6%
Small school	6%	5%
Small classes	5%	9%
Own child happy	2%	5%
Work ethic	0%	6%
Extra-curricular activities	0%	5%
Not too small	0%	2%
More traditional methods	0%	2%

to what might be termed the 'personal' side of a school, as evidenced by the high placings given to factors such as 'relationships', 'the staff' and, to a lesser extent, 'the headteacher'. The category of 'relationships', which was the single most frequently mentioned factor on both occasions, covers a wide range of interactions between the different participants in the life of a school, with a particular emphasis on those between teachers, children and parents. Key themes which recurred here were the sensitivity with which teachers responded to children and to parents, and the teachers' readiness to listen and explain. The following examples are typical of many:

> Relationships between parents and teachers. Two-way communication, particularly over problems.

Teachers who have time for children, who treat children as individuals.

Where parents and teachers can work together. Where teachers let you know what's going on.

The importance of the personal side of school life was also highlighted by the frequency of comments about 'the staff'. Here the emphasis was not so much on the relationships which teachers developed with parents and children, but more on their professional skills, motivation and dedication:

The teachers' ability, their enthusiasm, their capabilities. It's especially important in a small school if they can embrace all aspects, like science and music.

Good teachers that are prepared to work for the pupils and not just for the wage.

The important role of the headteacher was also mentioned, although less frequently than that of the staff. Moreover, the value of the head was seen primarily in terms of the effect which he or she had on the other teachers:

A very good head. It comes from the top.

A good head who makes sure standards are kept up. The teachers will work as hard as him [sic].

Table 6.1 also shows the priority which parents gave to the less tangible qualities of a school, such as its 'atmosphere' and 'ethos', compared with more tangible aspects such as 'resources', 'facilities' and 'small classes'. While there were indeed some parents who commented on the desirability of 'good equipment' or 'nice surroundings', there were many more who referred to the school's 'atmosphere' – that is, the feeling which a parent or visitor might obtain when walking along the corridors or venturing into a classroom:

A happy environment. The children are happy. There's an overall impression of politeness as you walk into the school.

> Kids are happy when you walk in. Paintings on the walls. Kids talk to you. Some noise, but no fighting.

> A friendly atmosphere, making them confident and relaxed, so they're not frightened to go to school.

While parents frequently mentioned that the school should have a happy atmosphere, there were very few explicit references to their own child's happiness. This might come as something of a surprise to the headteachers whom we interviewed in chapter 2. It will be recalled that when these heads were asked what their parents would consider 'makes a good school', the most frequent response was that parents were primarily interested in their own child's happiness (see table 2.3). The fact that this was rarely mentioned by the parents should not be taken as showing that they had no concern at all for their child's happiness: rather, as we have seen from the above examples, they were more concerned that a school should create a happy environment for all children, from which their own child – if he or she attended that school – would inevitably benefit.

The atmosphere created in a school is closely related to its 'ethos', another frequently mentioned factor. Here, though, the focus is more on the school's values or on what it is trying to accomplish:

> I like a school where the children are happy. Where the priority is on an interest in learning, rather than the academic side. There is anxiety in an achieving school.

> Not too strict but fairly pushy.

One important aspect of a school's ethos is its attitude to discipline, which was mentioned by over a quarter of the parents. For most of these parents the emphasis was not on discipline for its own sake, but as a means of ensuring that children could get on with the real purpose of schools, namely learning:

> Once you have discipline, you have an environment where everyone has a chance to get on. Otherwise their work will be affected.

You need to know that final discipline rests with the head. The children have got to know they will be protected. You can't learn if you're watching your back all the time.

At the same time, many parents felt that discipline had to be kept within certain limits:

Not too strict, mind.

or even, as one parent put it,

Discipline, but not capital [sic] punishment.

In keeping with the emphasis placed by parents on the more personal and less tangible aspects of a school was the low priority given to 'academic results', as well as the virtual absence of references to 'traditional methods'. Again, this might come as a surprise to the headteachers interviewed in chapter 2, who put 'traditional methods' in third place in their list of parents' criteria (see table 2.3). Moreover, many of the parents who did refer to 'results' or 'progress' did so in a relatively mild way, or combined it with other attributes of a good school:

I'd like to think my child is progressing.

A general atmosphere of enjoyment and busyness, coupled with reasonable discipline and fairly good results at the end of the day.

Although the number of parents who mentioned 'academic results' rose slightly over the two years, it was still similar to the number who mentioned 'developing the whole child' and lower than the number who referred to a 'wide ranging education'. As can be seen from the following examples, parents who mentioned the latter two factors were not necessarily ignoring the academic side of education, but were often situating it within a broader framework:

Children treated as individuals. Not in the sense of competition but stretched. It's a fine balance between pushing and undermining creativity.

Curriculum. That's what they're there for. You want to walk into a school and see projects on display, children doing constructive things, keeping busy, learning all sorts of things in a roundabout way.

Finally, table 6.1 shows there was virtually no change from Year 1 to Year 3 in the proportion of parents mentioning any particular factor. This may partly reflect the interviewing technique used in Year 3, when we repeated back to the parents what they had said in Year 1 and asked them if they still felt the same. It is possible that this technique has an in-built bias towards conformity, in that parents might find it easier simply to agree with what they said before rather than think through their position afresh. However, we did use the same technique on other occasions in our study, and were struck by the readiness with which parents were prepared to change their response, if they felt there had been a genuine change in their views. Our preferred interpretation is that the lack of change from Year 1 to Year 3 reflects an underlying stability in parents' beliefs about 'what makes a good school'.

Are parents happy with their child's school?

The parents were asked each year if they were happy with their child's school. Their responses were coded into one of five categories, ranging from 'very happy' to 'not happy', and then repeated back to them the following year. The distribution of the parents' responses over the three years is shown in table 6.2.

The overwhelming majority of parents each year were positive in their feelings about the school (see table 6.2). The combined total of parents who were either 'very happy', 'happy' or 'happy with reservations' was persistently high on each occasion – 87 per cent for Years 1 and 2 and 89 per cent for Year 3. These figures do not portray a group of parents who are seriously dissatisfied with their children's schools: on the contrary, they show a considerable and consistent degree of parental satisfaction.

Those parents who were essentially happy with the school tended

Table 6.2 Are parents happy with their child's school?

	Year 1 (n = 138)	Year 2 (n = 128)	Year 3 (n = 124)
Very happy	14%	13%	12%
Happy	62%	58%	54%
Happy with reservations	11%	16%	23%
Mixed feelings	10%	10%	8%
Not happy	4%	4%	2%

not to elaborate on why this was, beyond pointing out that their child was happy and making progress, and that they had no major cause for concern. The following two examples are typical of many satisfied parents:

Year 1   Yes, they seem to be doing alright.
Year 2   Very good indeed. They're progressing well.
Year 3   Still feel the same.

Year 1   Yes.
Year 2   Yes, even better. They had some staff changes which were a bit disruptive but it's much more stable now.
Year 3   I'm still very happy.

Some parents were more expansive:

Year 1   Yes, I'm very happy with the school.

Year 2   More than happy, even more so. There's lots of parents wanting children to go there, that speaks for itself. They had to take on extra teachers and have two more classes.

Year 3   The staff are very approachable, the head even more so. There's regular homework now, the teacher gives her as much as she wants. They've had a few trips lately to do with schoolwork, such as visiting a theatre workshop, and the children do enjoy them.

Some parents qualified their happiness by expressing one or more reservations. These reservations ranged over a number of topics and included concerns about progress, discipline, communication between home and school, a lack of response to complaints, the poor physical condition of the school, overcrowding and headlice. The reservations often concerned a particular incident or member of staff, and in many cases parents took pains to say that they were still happy with the school as a whole. As can be seen from table 6.2, there was a steady rise over the three years in the number of parents who expressed reservations, and a corresponding fall in the number of parents who simply said they were happy. This may merely reflect the fact that the parents became increasingly relaxed and talkative as the years went by, and may not reflect any major underlying change in their feelings about the school. Alternatively, it may be that after three years they had become more aware of the school's limitations, and so were more likely to express reservations. The following examples give some idea of typical reservations.

One parent had two older children at the school as well as the child we were following. She told us in Year 1 that she was happy with the school but expressed reservations in Years 2 and 3. These centred on her feeling that there was a discrepancy between the organization of the junior and infant departments; she did not have as much faith in the junior teachers as she did in the infant teachers. She based this on her experiences with her older children but only expressed it as a concern as her youngest child moved up the school.

Another parent expressed reservations in Year 3 about the school's handling of the transition from infant to junior classes. His son was one of the youngest in his year and had found it hard to settle to what was being expected of him. However, the parents had spoken to the teacher and were confident that their concerns would be addressed.

A third parent, who had been happy in the first two years, expressed reservations in the third year about the school's facilities and the state of the buildings. Her increasing concern about this aspect of the school was not due to any sudden deterioration in conditions since the last interview; rather it was because her daughter was now playing in the school football team and as a result she had visited other local schools and been able to make comparisons.

The vast majority of parents were clearly happy with their child's school. However, there were some parents each year who had 'mixed feelings' or said they were 'not happy' with the school. Typically, their concerns were similar to the reservations just described, but were expressed in stronger terms. Some of these parents had considered moving their child, or had actually done so, and we will look at them more closely later in this chapter.

Do parents think teachers do a good job?

Another way in which we attempted to measure parents' satisfaction with their child's school was by asking them whether they thought the teachers at the school were, on the whole, doing a good job. As with other questions, their responses were repeated back to them in subsequent interviews, and they were asked if they still felt the same. This question acquired particular significance in view of the importance which the parents attached to the teachers' role when answering the question 'what makes a good school?', as we saw earlier in this chapter. Our intention was that the question should refer to the teaching staff as a whole, and most parents did indeed seem to answer it in these terms. There were a few parents, however, who really only knew about their child's teacher (particularly in Year 1) and who therefore based their response on that teacher. The parents' responses were coded into one of six main categories, and the distribution of responses over the three years is shown in table 6.3.

The great majority of parents spoke positively about the teachers at their child's school. As table 6.3 shows, the combined total of parents who thought the teachers' performance was either 'excellent', 'good' or 'good with reservations' was persistently high across the three years – ranging from 83 per cent in Year 1 to 90 per cent in Year 2 and 88 per cent in Year 3. A comparison with table 6.2 suggests that, if anything, the parents' responses to this question were even more positive than their responses to the previous one, with more parents responding in the most positive

Table 6.3 Do parents think teachers do a good job?

	Year 1 (n = 138)	Year 2 (n = 128)	Year 3 (n = 124)
Excellent job	17%	31%	27%
Good job	54%	45%	48%
Good with reservations	12%	14%	13%
Mixed feelings	10%	6%	10%
Not sure/don't know	5%	2%	1%
Not doing a good job	1%	2%	2%

category (particularly in Years 2 and 3) and fewer parents expressing reservations.

As with the previous question, many parents did not spontaneously amplify their responses, particularly if they were positive. Thus there were many parents who simply replied 'yes', 'very good', 'excellent' or even 'brilliant'. But there were also many parents who gave justifications for why they had answered as they did, and these justifications provide interesting insights into the criteria which the parents were using to judge the teachers' performance.

One major theme in the parents' comments was that a good teacher is lively, enthusiastic and stimulates the children with interesting activities:

> They're very enthusiastic about things. They're doing lots of different things with them and going on lots of trips.

> Lots of novel ideas which the children seem to enjoy. My daughter loves projects, to be given an idea and to come up with something or the results herself.

> I'm very impressed with the headteacher. There's a real feeling of enthusiasm.

The corollary is that teachers were sometimes criticized for failing to stimulate the children or for providing work which was insufficiently challenging:

I think that children who are not so bright could be pushed harder. My youngest is OK: she's bright and I'm happy with her progress. But the twins are just plodding along. They need extra help with the 11-plus coming up.

The reading books are too easy. He brings the same one home and it's too easy.

He finishes his work quite quickly, and when he comes out of school he is so wound up. He has so much physical and mental energy.

A second common theme was the emphasis parents placed on the quality of relationships which teachers were building with the children and their parents. This, of course, echoes the importance parents attached to 'relationships' when asked 'what makes a good school?' earlier in the chapter. Again this was expressed both positively and negatively. Parents were quick to point out when they felt that teachers were particularly caring, or when they seemed to be working hard to build relationships:

They're very good. They seem to care about the children. From the very first day they bring books home.

They are very caring teachers. There's a good parent–teacher relationship.

I think her teacher is brilliant. She's been very sensitive to her particular needs, as she's had a lot of upheaval in her life.

At the same time, parents were also ready to point out when they felt teachers were not giving children enough individual attention, or when they were failing to communicate adequately with parents:

The teachers don't have time for the children.

There is a problem with the parent–teacher relationship. You never know what's going on.

It wasn't until we had the reports that we knew something was the matter.

A third dimension which was important to parents was the extent to which teachers exerted discipline and maintained control of the classroom. Some parents appeared to equate good teaching with good discipline:

> The children seem under control now. They're better behaved. Even the infants are under more control.

> The teachers are trying but it's not easy for them. It's a mixed-age group and the older children play up and disrupt.

Similarly, lack of control or ineffective management techniques in both classroom and playground were sometimes cited as a sign of a 'bad' teacher:

> They don't keep tabs on the children. Children lose things at school. They come home with ripped clothes or their glasses knocked off.

> They are good teachers if they would sort out the problems but they say 'just get on with it'. That's no way to go on.

and even

> Some teachers get a bit carried away with shouting and that. You can hear them when they're stuck out in the playground.

Finally, it was clear that many parents were aware of the disruptions which schools were facing because of the National Curriculum and other aspects of the educational reforms. Parents became particularly concerned when staff shortages or in-service training meant their children were taught by a succession of different teachers, and several parents felt that schools could do more to minimize the disruption this caused. At the same time, there was a widespread awareness of the pressure and stress teachers were experiencing, and a genuine appreciation of how well teachers were coping in difficult circumstances. Many parents were also aware of the strained financial situation which many schools found themselves in, and that the lack of resources and facilities was not necessarily the school's fault:

They do a good job with limited resources.

Brilliant under difficult circumstances.

and the somewhat ambiguous

They do a wonderful job considering the limitations they have.

Are parents happy with their children's progress?

The third way we assessed parents' satisfaction was by asking them whether they were happy with their child's progress in the three core subjects of the National Curriculum – English, maths and science. These questions were only asked in Year 2, for the following reasons. At the time of the Year 1 interviews, some of the children had only been in school for just over a term, so we felt it was too early to ask parents about their children's progress, while in the Year 3 interviews questions about progress were part of a more detailed set of questions about assessment (see chapter 9). For the purposes of this question, English was divided into the three principal profile components of *reading, writing* and *speaking and listening*. The parents' responses are shown in table 6.4.

The great majority of parents were evidently happy with their

Table 6.4 Are parents happy with their child's progress? (Year 2, $n = 128$.)

	Reading	Writing	Speaking/ listening	Maths	Science
Yes	80%	80%	79%	79%	45%
Mixed feelings	9%	13%	14%	8%	0%
No	11%	6%	4%	4%	0%
Don't know enough about it	0%	1%	2%	9%	52%

children's progress in the '3Rs' – that is, reading, writing and maths. These parents typically commented that their children were doing well, and in some cases that they were performing even better than expected. Many children were also said to be enjoying their work in these subjects, particularly in the area of maths. Some parents, however, were less than fully satisfied. This was particularly evident in the area of reading, with several parents expressing concern about their children's progress.

The parents' responses to the science question were very different from their responses about English and maths (see table 6.4). All the parents who gave an opinion about science said they were satisfied with their children's progress, and many of these parents commented that their children found it interesting and enjoyable. However, just over half the parents said they were unable to give an opinion as they did not know enough about it. Some of these parents pointed out that science was a very new subject, and that they had little or no idea of what was expected of young children in this area. Other parents were adamant that their children did not do science at all, although we knew from the schools that this was not the case.

The parents' responses to these questions raise a number of important issues which we will take up again later. In chapter 7, for example, we will look more closely at what parents thought their children should be learning in these areas of the curriculum; in chapter 8 we will return to the issue of how much they knew about what their children were doing in school, while in chapter 9 we will examine what the parents learnt about their children's progress from the standardized assessments which took place at the end of Year 2. Meanwhile, we will look in the next section at those parents who were so unhappy about their children's progress that they considered moving them to another school.

Would parents move their child to another school?

Our final measure of parental satisfaction was whether parents were sufficiently unhappy that they considered moving their child to another school, and whether any parents actually did so. This measure is particularly relevant to parents' role as consumers: as we saw earlier, the right of parents to leave a school they were unhappy with and try elsewhere was mentioned both by parents and by headteachers as being an important aspect of the consumer's role. This issue is also extremely relevant to the success of the current educational reforms: one of the assumptions underlying the reforms is that parents will leave a school which is under-performing and transfer their custom to one which is more successful. We were therefore interested to find out how far parents would operate like this in practice.

In the first interview we explored with the parents the extent to which moving their child was a possibility. We asked whether they would consider moving their child to another school, and if so, what would make them do this. The great majority of parents said they would consider moving their child if necessary, although for nearly a third this was only something they would contemplate as a last resort. The most frequently stated reasons were if their child was unhappy, if their child was not making adequate progress, if the teaching was unsatisfactory, or if their child was being bullied. Many parents, however, said they would first try to sort things out with the teacher. Other parents commented that such a move might be very disruptive for the child, that there was no guarantee they would be better off elsewhere, or that they had no real alternative to the current school. Nevertheless, despite these caveats, it was clear that most parents would at least consider moving their child if the situation warranted it.

In subsequent years we looked at the extent to which this possibility had become a reality. We asked the parents if at any point in the previous year they had considered moving their child, and if so, what had caused them to do this. We also asked whether any parents had actually moved their child to another school, and why they had done so. Parents who were forced to move their child because they were leaving the area or because their children were required to move to the junior school (see chapter 3) were excluded from this analysis. The responses given by the remaining parents are shown in table 6.5.

The great majority of parents did not consider moving their child during the period of the study (see table 6.5). In almost all

Table 6.5 Had parents considered moving or actually moved their child?

	Year 2 (n = 124)	Year 3 (n = 110)
Not considered moving child	81%	85%
Considered moving child but didn't	18%	13%
Actually moved child	1%	2%

cases the reason was simple: they were happy with the school and saw no need to think about moving. As in Year 1, some parents commented that they would try to sort it out first, that such a move would be too disruptive for the child, that there was no guarantee things would be better elsewhere, or that there simply was no realistic alternative to the current school.

About one in six parents had at some stage in the previous year considered moving their child but had not in fact done so (see table 6.5). These parents mentioned that their child had been unhappy or had not been making progress, or that they were concerned about the teaching or about discipline, or that they were generally dissatisfied with the school. The parents also gave reasons why they had not actually gone through with the move. As before, some said it would be too disruptive for the child, or that there was no guarantee things would be better elsewhere. However, most of these parents said that things had been sorted out or had spontaneously improved, and that they were no longer considering moving their child. The following examples give some idea of the concerns expressed by parents in this group.

One family lived some distance from the school their son attended, although they had chosen it in preference to the nearest school for which he would have had free transport. By the second interview the father was ill and unable to work. This had caused some upheaval in the family, as the mother had to cope with hospital visiting as well as school runs. She was also unhappy about the way the school was teaching her son to read, and felt a lot was being left to chance. The mother had mentioned her concerns to the teacher, who had told her that if she heard every child read every day it would take four hours a day. It was at this point that the mother thought about moving her son to another school. By the time of the interview she had decided not to do this, as she felt the situation had been somewhat resolved: the teacher was now hearing her son read more often, although the mother did worry about the other children in the class.

Another parent was concerned about his child's lack of progress. His wife was a supply teacher, and they had decided that until she had a permanent job they would not move the children as the school was conveniently situated. The father felt that the head was wary of him as he voiced his concerns and was active on the Parent Teacher Association. Between Years 2 and 3 the parents became involved in a dispute with the school about their middle daughter's progress. This had resulted in her being moved into another class and this seemed to have solved the problem as she was making good progress; however, the parents now had concerns about the youngest daughter, and felt unable to communicate with her teacher about these concerns. We subsequently heard after the final interview that the parents had eventually moved both children to another school.

The third parent was concerned about bullying and for this reason was considering moving her two children. She felt her son was being blamed for things he had not done, and that there were 'too many bullies in his class and a lot of friction during school time'. She felt the school did not ask questions about who started things. She had enquired about another school but the headteacher had said she would take one child but not the other, and the mother did not feel it was right to split them up. The headteacher at this other school had also said she would contact her if two places became available. The parent commented that, although she had been to look at the other school, she did not feel it was any better than the current one.

A few parents actually moved their children during the course of the study (see table 6.5). Two parents moved their children into the private sector, while three moved within the state sector. We will describe the circumstances of each move in some detail.

One of the parents who moved into the private sector had always intended to do this, as her older child was already at the private school. This parent was the widow of an Army officer and various trust funds were helping her with school fees. One of the main advantages of the private school was that she could leave her children there until 6 pm if necessary, thus enabling her to return to work. She took great pains to say how satisfied she had been with the state primary school.

The other set of parents who moved into the private sector went through several changes during the course of the study. At the time of the first interview they were running a home for the mentally disabled, and their children attended the village school; they were generally happy with the school but concerned about their daughter's progress in maths. Soon after this interview they moved their children to a private school about 15 miles away, as they felt nothing had been done about their daughter's lack of progress; they commented that in no time at all their children were making great strides at the private school. Shortly after this the parents gave up running the home and moved to another town, where they opened a shop. This meant that their children had to board at the private school, and their son in particular was very unhappy with this. The parents therefore moved their children, with some reluctance, to another private school nearer the town where they were now living. By the time of the third interview things had changed again. The parents had become very unhappy with the second private school, claiming the headmistress had called their son 'stupid' to his face, and had moved the children back to the original private school. They had also given up the shop as the father had not been able to cope with the work. However, despite these changes in their own lives the parents stated their determination to give their children the best chance possible, and were very keen to keep them at their current private school. It was not clear what would happen next.

Three parents moved their children from one state school to another. One of these lived on the edge of a small town. She had sent her two sons to a school in a nearby village because it was a church school and was also smaller than the local primary school. At the time of the first interview she was happy with her choice, although she commented that she did not like the school's reading scheme. Three weeks before the second interview the parent had moved both her sons to the local primary school. She had done this over the autumn half-term, but had not told the children until they were taken to their new school on the first day after the holiday. Her reason for the change had been the younger child's lack of progress, particularly in learning his letter sounds. She said the school had not informed her until shortly before the move that he did not know his sounds, although he had been kept in the reception class when his peer group had moved up into the next class. She commented during this second interview that he 'never had a reading book home at the old school, but now he was bringing home two a night'. She wished she had moved him earlier but she did not realize anything was wrong. She was still happy a year later when her son had moved on to the junior school, but still felt that the original school had let her and her son down.

The second set of parents who moved within the state sector were interviewed together in the first year of the project. They had recently moved to the area in order to buy their own council house, and the father had set up his own coal business. They were not happy with the school during that first interview and wanted to move their son to another school. During the second interview the mother was not very forthcoming, but still expressed the desire that her son should change schools, and said that he wanted to do so as well. However, apart from saying that he was a tearaway, she did not seem to be unhappy about his progress. By the time of the final interview her son had moved to the new school and had settled well. All the same, it was still very difficult to elicit what her dissatisfactions had been with the original school. She said the teachers had been sorry to see her son go and had given him a lovely report.

The third set of parents who moved within the state system lived on a large inner-city council estate. The school which their son initially attended had not been their first choice, but had been the only one which would take him. They had been refused by their first choice, a Catholic school which the father had attended, because the son had not been christened, and by another state school because the family lived outside the school's catchment area. During the first interview the mother expressed her unease about the school. She had always done lots of educational activities with her son at home and felt she knew his capabilities: consequently, she was alarmed when the same reading book kept coming home despite her son reading it perfectly to her. She was also concerned because he had not started doing sums at school, despite having done plenty at home. At the second interview the mother was even more concerned about her son's schooling. In addition to continued lack of progress, she said her son had become the target of bullying, coming home with his clothes ripped and bruising on his neck, and was reluctant to go to school. The mother had been told by a friend who worked as a dinner lady at the Catholic school that if the school had known that the father had attended as a child then they would have looked more favourably upon the son, despite his not being christened. Shortly after this second interview her son was in fact admitted to the Catholic school. At the time of the final interview the mother was very happy with the new school: she felt her son was making good progress and that the teachers were keen to keep parents informed about what was happening in the classroom.

The examples given in this section suggest there is no single reason why parents consider moving their children from one school to another, or why they actually do so. Although concern about children's lack of progress appeared to be the most common reason, it was not the only one – children's unhappiness, bullying, lack of discipline, and poor teaching were also mentioned. A further factor which seemed to be involved was the way in which the school had responded to such concerns. If the parents' concerns had been dealt with in a sympathetic and sensitive fashion, then it was more than likely that the parents would stay; conversely, if the school had ignored the parents' concerns or responded insensitively, then it increased the chances that the parents would leave. In addition, as the case studies show, out-of-school factors are often involved as well, such as changing circumstances in the parents' own lives.

These examples of parental dissatisfaction amongst a small minority of parents need to be set in the broader context of general satisfaction amongst the great majority of parents. Indeed, the picture emerging from all the measures of satisfaction used in this chapter is broadly similar: while there are clearly some parents who have concerns and dissatisfactions, these concerns are by no means widespread. On the contrary, it appears that the great majority of parents are happy with the school, think teachers are doing a good job, are happy with their child's progress and would not consider moving their child to another school.

Are parents concerned about 'standards' in state education?

It was suggested at the start of this chapter that many parents might be satisfied with their own child's school but have wider concerns about 'standards' in state education more generally. We investigated this possibility by asking the parents in the Year 2 interviews if they were concerned about 'standards' in state education. In the period leading up to this interview there had been a lot of media reports about falling standards, particularly in the area of reading, and we made explicit reference to these in our question. We pointed out that there had been a lot of talk in the papers about standards in state education, and asked the parents if they had any major concerns themselves.

The parents were much more concerned about 'standards' in state education generally than they were about their own child's school. As figure 6.1 shows, over half the parents expressed either 'major' or 'minor' concerns about standards in general: this contrasts with the relatively small proportion of parents who were dissatisfied with their own child's school. The most frequently expressed concern about 'standards' was with the level of basic skills, especially reading; in addition, parents expressed concerns

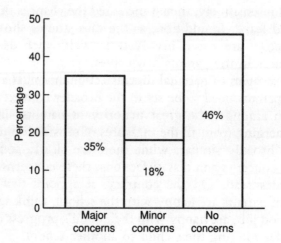

Figure 6.1 Are parents concerned about 'standards' in state education? (Year 2, *n* = 127.)

about teachers not pushing children hard enough and about discipline. At the same time, many parents qualified their response by saying they had no concerns about standards in their own child's school, or with their own child's progress. The following comment was typical of such parents:

> I do worry that standards are falling. This is something I've just picked up in general, not because of my own children. English and maths are the most important. If there isn't a thorough grounding in these then the future can be affected.

The following parent, in contrast, explicitly connected his concerns about standards in general to the progress of his own child. As his comments suggest, he had no actual evidence that his child was making poor progress: it was more that the attention given in the media to 'falling standards' had led him to wonder whether in fact she was falling behind:

> I suppose I do have concerns about standards. Ground lost at her age will be hard to regain later. It does concern me. She may have lost ground without us realizing it at the time.

Many parents seemed to feel there was indeed something going wrong 'out there', but they were not too sure what it was. As one parent put it:

> It's very difficult to assess what exactly is going on. There are so many changes at the moment that it's difficult to put your finger on what is going wrong. I've no major concerns with my own child. Hopefully, this is where assessment will help to spot where things are going wrong.

Another parent said, somewhat sorrowfully:

> There's something sadly missing in schools altogether.

Such comments raise the question of how parents have arrived at this kind of opinion. Many of them made it clear that their main source of information – as was implied by our original question – was the media. At the same time, several parents seemed unsure about how much weight to put on media accounts about standards, and some felt they were being manipulated by the media for an underlying political purpose:

> It's been very one-sided publicity. It causes a lot of anxiety in parents. It's so negative I wonder if it's been rigged. They don't give a proper balance. You don't hear children's point of view. It all fits in with the policy they want to push through. I feel as if I'm being manipulated.

Overview

In this chapter we have looked at what the parents considered to make a good school, whether they were satisfied with their own child's school and whether they had wider concerns about 'standards' in state education. While there are undoubtedly some important variations between parents on these issues, there is nevertheless a clear consensus on a number of points.

First, we found little evidence to support the idea that there is widespread dissatisfaction amongst parents with their children's schools. The picture which emerged from our four measures of parental satisfaction was in fact remarkably similar. At least 80 per cent of the parents were happy with their child's school, thought that the teachers were doing a good job, were happy with their child's progress in the 3Rs, and had not considered moving their child to another school. These figures, it should be noted, fit closely with research carried out before the National Curriculum was introduced and cited at the start of this chapter. This in turn indicates that the high levels of satisfaction which we found cannot be ascribed simply to the arrival of the National Curriculum.

Second, we gained some insight into the criteria which parents use to judge a school and its teachers. Their responses when asked 'what makes a good school' suggest that they placed more emphasis on the personal and less tangible aspects of school life – such as relationships, the staff, the ethos and the atmosphere – than they did on aspects such as resources, facilities or academic results. They also considered a good teacher to be one who was lively, enthusiastic and stimulating, who built up good relationships with children and parents and who maintained control in the classroom and playground. Furthermore, the great majority of parents felt that these criteria were being met by their children's schools and their teachers.

We also gained some insight into the circumstances under which parents might consider moving their child to another school, and why some would actually do this. The most frequently mentioned reasons for considering a move were if their child was unhappy or not making progress; in addition, whether parents actually moved their child depended, among other things, on how well such problems were dealt with by the school. While the emphasis in such decisions on their child's happiness and progress may not at first sight fit with the criteria parents use to judge a school and its teachers, the contradiction is more apparent than real. If a school and its teachers met the parents' criteria, then it is more than likely that their children would be happy and making progress; if they did not, then the converse would be true.

Finally, while the parents were generally satisfied with their own child's school, over half of them expressed concerns about 'standards' in state education more generally. This is a curious phenomenon which deserves closer scrutiny. The most obvious explanation is that parents were drawing on two very different kinds of experience when answering these questions. On the subject of their child's school, they could rely on direct observation and experience: they could see their children were happy and making progress, and that the teachers were working hard to maintain standards. But when asked about standards in general, they were forced to rely on what they had learnt from the media – which at the time were carrying a number of stories suggesting that standards were falling. Whether such stories were a true reflection of what was actually happening in schools is, of course, another matter.

7

Parents and the National Curriculum

I approve of the concept but not of what's happening in schools, especially the amount of work engendered.

(Parent's comments on the National Curriculum)

The centre-piece of the current educational reforms is the National Curriculum itself. Introduced by the 1988 Education Reform Act, the National Curriculum specifies what will be taught to all children from the ages of 5 to 16 years in all schools in England and Wales. A particular emphasis is given to the three 'core' subjects of English, maths and science, although pupils must also learn the seven 'foundation' subjects of history, geography, technology, art, music, PE and (for secondary pupils only) a foreign language. Each of these ten subjects is broken down into specific areas, or Attainment Targets, and various National Curriculum documents set out what is to be achieved within each Attainment Target at each of ten broad levels.

It is widely assumed that the National Curriculum has been greeted with strong approval from the great majority of parents. Certainly, its potential advantages have been explicitly pointed out to them in a series of government leaflets and pamphlets produced for their benefit. For example, a pamphlet entitled 'Our Changing Schools: A Handbook for Parents' produced by the Department of Education and Science in 1988 stated clearly that:

The National Curriculum is designed to help raise standards for all pupils. It will be brought in over the next few years. It means that your child will receive a broad, balanced education throughout primary school – but one which is based on his or her needs. (p. 11)

A later document from the same source, entitled 'Your Child and the National Curriculum', elaborated on these advantages in more detail:

> The National Curriculum guarantees that all children will be taught what they really need to know, with checks on their progress at every stage. This means that you as a parent can find out what your child is doing at school and why. . . . This combination of clear targets and national tests will help ensure that:
>
> - teachers have the highest possible expectations of their pupils
> - standards are raised in schools right across the country
> - pupils can move from one school to another without disrupting their education
> - you, as a parent, can hold your child's school to account for the progress your child is making and for the standards of the school generally. (Department of Education and Science, 1991b, pp. 2–3)

The idea that parents approve of the National Curriculum was certainly shared by the majority of headteachers in our telephone survey (see chapter 2). These heads thought that their parents supported the National Curriculum on the grounds that it would lead to higher educational standards, either in their own child's school or in the country more generally. At the same time, many of the heads felt that parents' attitudes towards the National Curriculum had been strongly influenced by outside sources, such as the media or the school itself, while a few heads thought that parents were not sufficiently interested to have an opinion.

The parents in our study were particularly well placed to offer their views on these issues. Their children were among the first cohort to experience the National Curriculum at Key Stage One (5–7 years), and they were also among the first group of children to be assessed at the age of 7 years. The parents were thus able to experience at first hand the effects of the National Curriculum and assessment on their children and their schools. What the parents have to say about these innovations is therefore of particular importance.

In this chapter, we will look at the parents' attitude towards the National Curriculum itself. We focus on the following questions:

- Do parents approve or disapprove of the National Curriculum?
- Are they happy with the emphasis it places on English, maths and science?
- What do parents think should be taught in these subjects?
- What importance do they attach to the other foundation subjects such as history, geography and technology?

In the next chapter we will look at how much the parents knew about the National Curriculum and other developments within the school, while in chapter 9 we focus on the controversial issue of assessment.

Parents' attitude to the National Curriculum

Each year the parents were asked if they approved or disapproved of the National Curriculum. As can be seen from figure 7.1, the parents were generally in favour of the National Curriculum, but not overwhelmingly so. The proportion of parents who approved of the National Curriculum increased slowly during the period of the study, but was still only just over 50 per cent in Year 3. There was a steady fall over the years in the number of parents who said that they didn't know enough about the National Curriculum to give an opinion, as well as a corresponding rise in the number of parents saying they had mixed feelings. Only a small number of parents each year registered a straightforward disapproval of the National Curriculum.

A similar picture emerged from the parents' responses to another question in which they were asked what were the main advantages and disadvantages of the National Curriculum. This question was asked in Year 1, where the emphasis was more on the idea of a national curriculum in general, as well as in Year 3, where the emphasis was more on the National Curriculum which had actually been introduced. As can be seen from figure 7.2

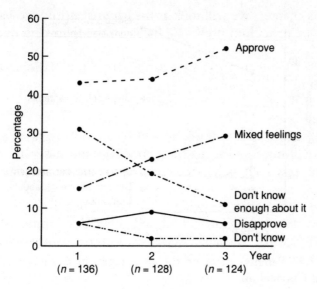

Figure 7.1   Do parents approve or disapprove of the National Curriculum?

(on page 128) the most frequent response on each occasion was for parents to mention *both* advantages and disadvantages, particularly in Year 3. Of those who only gave advantages or disadvantages, there were around three times as many parents in the former category as in the latter.

The picture which emerges from both these questions is one of qualified support for the National Curriculum. While parents were much more likely to be in favour of the National Curriculum than opposed to it, there were still many parents who either had mixed feelings towards it or who could see that it had both advantages and disadvantages. In order to understand this ambivalence, we need to look more closely at what parents thought were the benefits of the National Curriculum, and at their concerns.

Benefits of the National Curriculum

The benefits which parents thought would result from the National Curriculum fell into three main categories – benefits for teachers, benefits for children and benefits for parents.

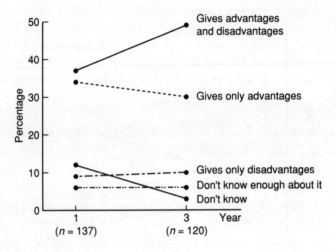

Figure 7.2 Parents' views on the advantages/disadvantages of the National Curriculum.

The main benefit for teachers was that their job would be made simpler and clearer by having an explicit set of guidelines spelling out what would be taught and when it would be taught. These guidelines would help teachers overcome differences in their training, experience or skills, so that they would all be equally competent at putting over a broad and balanced curriculum:

> It will be helpful for new teachers. It will help them to know that everyone has the same aims.

> It's easier for teachers to work with guidelines. Most teachers have always had one – it's just never been put into words.

and even

> It's good for those teachers who aren't well organized.

The main benefit for children, according to the parents, was that the National Curriculum would add an increased element of fairness to the education system. By setting out what should be taught at a particular age, children would not be subjected to the vagaries or idiosyncrasies of particular teachers or schools; by specifying the range of subjects to be introduced, the National Curriculum would make sure that no children missed out in a particular area; and by making explicit what the progression was within a particular subject, the National Curriculum would ensure that children would not waste time repeating work or attempting work at the wrong level for them. Parents also thought that children would be less likely to suffer if they had time off school for illness, or if they moved schools. This underlying idea of increased fairness for children is made with varying degrees of explicitness in the following comments:

It will give everyone a fair chance.

It's a good idea, getting children to compete on equal terms.

It will avoid repetition from one year to the next.

It will encourage children to do well. It will stop them sitting around doing nothing at lower grades.

If they move then their education can just carry on – they won't slip back but just slot in.

The third group who were seen as benefiting were the parents themselves. By setting out what their children were supposed to be learning at each level in each subject, the National Curriculum would make it much easier for parents to find out what they were doing, to get some idea of whether they were making adequate progress, and to provide help where necessary:

Parents will know more about children's progression and can become more involved.

It will be good for parents to know what the aim is so they can help.

Parents will know exactly where children are with their work. It can only be better from the parents' point of view.

Concerns about the National Curriculum

The parents' concerns about the National Curriculum fell into two main areas – concerns about the principle of the National Curriculum, and concerns about the way it had been implemented in practice.

The main concern expressed about the principle of the National Curriculum was that it was too restrictive – both on teachers and on children. Many parents felt it was important, particularly at this age, that there should be an element of spontaneity, creativity, and even fun in education. They were concerned that this might be lost if the curriculum laid down precisely what children should be doing at any particular moment:

> It could be too rigid. It doesn't allow work to progress organically.

> The good things in schools are threatened by it. It kills the fun things.

> I worry whether it's too rigid, especially with infants. If they're channelled too much it will detract from what they're doing – like in their writing. They'd lose the creativity.

> I hope it doesn't get parrot fashion. They need basics but to develop in their own way.

The other main area of concern was with the way in which the National Curriculum had been introduced in practice. These concerns took a number of forms. Some parents were concerned that there might be too much to fit in to the school day. They were aware that a number of new subjects were being introduced, and were not aware that anything was being taken out of the curriculum to enable this to happen:

> There's not enough time to do everything well enough. There's too short a time for so many subjects.

Concerns were also expressed about the pace with which change had been introduced, and the resulting stress this seemed to have caused. Many parents were aware of the increased workload which the National Curriculum had meant for teachers, and some felt that insufficient resources had been made available for teachers to do the job properly. Several parents pointed out that those introducing the changes had failed to carry the teachers with them, and that this was inherently unsatisfactory. This last point was made particularly clearly by the following parent:

> I've listened to the teachers and they don't approve, so why should we? If they can't sell it to teachers how can they sell it to us?

As we saw earlier, there were many parents who pointed out both positive and negative features of the National Curriculum. Indeed, there were some parents who took advantage of our interviews to carry out a private debate with themselves on the issues involved, putting forward the arguments first for one side and then for the other. Perhaps the best example of this comes from the following parent, who was a youth worker and a lay preacher. Although not directly involved in education himself, he seemed well acquainted with many of the issues involved:

Year 1 *Do you approve or disapprove of the National Curriculum?*
I'm in two minds. If it was going ahead slower I'd be happier. It's too fast. My nightmare is that it will not be worked out properly. But in principle, yes.

What do you see as its advantages?
It will allow central monitoring of standards. It will prevent waste of pupil time on irrelevant issues such as political sympathies of staff. It allows debate nationally.

And the disadvantages?
The inflexibility. The difficulty of making it work in so many situations, needs and different levels of ability. Having a National Curriculum allows more effective political interference. There's also a tendency to say that if something isn't in the National Curriculum, then it doesn't exist.

Year 2   *Do you still feel the same?*
Yes, I've still got mixed feelings. The schools have reacted amazingly well. It was a tall order – in fact it still is. The first lot of testing will be telling – although GCSE results show you can still get results without proper resourcing. I feel the National Curriculum will give benefits in some kind of way. It was too much too soon, but we're still coming to terms with it. It's changing peoples' attitude in the teaching profession. It's introduced accountability. Life feels more purposeful. On the other hand, I worry about the fact that if something's not in the National Curriculum then it doesn't exist. I worry about the position of Religious Education. If something's not central it gets swept to the sidelines.

Year 3   *Do you still feel the same?*
Yes, I think so. I've still got mixed feelings. RE is still in a strange situation. Overall, it's double-edged. It could be useful but capable of political manipulation. They're trying to traditionalize things. The National Curriculum is giving politicians a handle on education, taking it away from educationalists.

What do you see as its advantages?
It gives some kind of shaping. It gives the same kind of assessment between schools. They can't spend 90 per cent of their time on peace studies. It's sharpened up questions about what children should be learning. It provides the means to see how a school is doing.

And the disadvantages?
The main one is that it's open to manipulation.

It would be misleading to suggest that all the parents in our study engaged in such lengthy debates on this issue. Nevertheless, it would not be misleading to suggest that this kind of ambivalence was fairly common, even among parents who basically approved of the National Curriculum. Indeed, the parents' feelings towards the National Curriculum could best be summed up as 'good in theory, but problematic in practice'.

Table 7.1   Do parents think English, maths and science are the most important aspects of the curriculum?

	Year 1 (n = 137)	Year 2 (n = 127)	Year 3 (n = 124)
Yes	61%	60%	60%
Yes, but not the only ones	21%	24%	26%
Yes, but not so much science	16%	13%	12%
No	1%	2%	2%

Parents and the core curriculum

One of the most important features of the National Curriculum is the clear emphasis it places on English, maths and science. These three subjects are explicitly defined as forming the 'core' of the curriculum, and have been given particular prominence in the standardized assessments. In this respect, the National Curriculum can be seen as responding to a widespread concern that more attention should be given to the 'basics'. Given that parents are generally considered to share this concern for basics, it might well be assumed that they would approve of the pre-eminence given to these particular subjects.

We asked the parents each year whether they thought that English, maths and science were the most important aspects of the curriculum. As table 7.1 shows, the majority of parents were happy with the priority given to these subjects. Many of these parents answered the question by simply saying 'yes', giving few explanations for their response. There were two main ways, however, in which parents qualified a positive reply.

The most frequent qualification, produced by about a quarter of the parents, was that the three core subjects should not become too important and crowd out other things. This point was well summed up by the following parent:

They're basic, but not overriding.

Other parents expressed their concern that the preoccupation with basic skills might take attention from what they felt were more fundamental values in education, such as discovery, creativity or even enjoyment. In this respect they were echoing concerns expressed earlier about the National Curriculum in general:

> Basic literacy and numeracy are important, but what's most important is to get children to enjoy learning and find it interesting. They should be doing things, finding things out for themselves.

> I'm worried that other things will be put aside for these three subjects – there'll be no fun at school.

> I know they're important ingredients but I do think there should be much more emphasis on creative activities, like music and painting. You see so little enjoyment even in infant schools – there's all that pressure now to get a tick. There's so much to be learned that hasn't been acknowledged. A sense of self – putting yourself across in a way. They're only using one part of the brain with this curriculum.

A few parents expressed their regret that a foreign language was not being taught at this age. One parent mentioned that it was easier for children to learn another language at the age of 5 than when they were older, while another commented that 'other European countries have the advantage on us as they start children earlier on languages'.

The other main qualification was to say that, while English and maths were important, the same priority should not be given to science. This was perhaps not surprising, as the particular prominence given to science is very much a novel feature of the National Curriculum. This qualification was expressed particularly graphically by one parent, who commented that 'English and maths come before any Bunsen burners'.

The number of parents who felt that science was not as important as English and maths declined slowly over the three years (see table 7.1). The comments given by some of the parents who changed their responses suggests that they were strongly influenced by the interest their child had shown in science during Key Stage One. The following parent, for example, stated quite clearly

in Years 1 and 2 that English and maths were much more important than science, but by Year 3 she had revised her opinion:

Year 1   I don't think science is that important. Maths and English,
         yes.

Year 2   I still feel the same. You can get on if you can read and
         write and do maths. Science is only important if you want
         to go into medicine or biochemistry.

Year 3   I think science should be a big part of it. Children didn't
         do it before. We never did it, but going by what he said,
         he enjoyed it so much. It gives them other things to think
         about.

Another parent who was initially less than enthusiastic about
science also changed her mind when she learnt more about what
it involved. This parent came to see that science at this age need
not be a totally separate subject, but that it can involve elements
of other subjects:

Year 2   Seeing science in practice made me realize how much
         English and maths comes into science. They add things
         together, and write up what they've done. I've become
         more positive about science. It's creeping up on me!

Most of the parents, then, were happy that English, maths and
science should be given priority in the early years of education. In
that sense, parents were clearly supporting the emphasis on the
'basics' which is implied by placing these subjects at the core of
the National Curriculum. But there is another sense in which
parents are frequently thought to favour a return to the basics:
namely, that they would like to see more emphasis on 'traditional
methods' for teaching these subjects. This perception of parents
was certainly shared by many of the headteachers in our telephone
survey, over a third of whom said that the use of 'traditional
methods' was one of the criteria by which parents judged a school
(see table 2.3). In other words, it might be assumed that parents
would want to see a greater use of formal methods, more whole-
class teaching, and more emphasis on spelling tests and the memor-
izing of multiplication tables.

In view of the increasing attention being given to these issues in public debate (e.g. Alexander, Rose and Woodhead, 1992), we wanted to find out whether the parents in our study had strong views on what should be taught in the three core subjects and on what teaching methods should be used. We approached this issue in two main ways. In Year 1, we asked the parents what they thought their child should be taught in English, maths and science; we then asked if this was what their child was actually being taught in that subject. In Year 2 we asked the parents if there was anything in the methods used or work covered in the core subjects that the parent 'found surprising'. This particular phrase was chosen because we thought it might focus the parent's mind on any discrepancies between what they would ideally like to see in a school and what was actually going on in their child's school.

Neither of these approaches turned out to be entirely satisfactory. One reason was that, as we shall see in the next chapter, many parents had only a limited knowledge of what was going on in their child's classroom, and so found it difficult to answer questions about what their child was *currently* being taught or about the methods being used. But another, and perhaps more surprising, reason was that parents were often just as vague about what they thought *should* be taught. We had expected that parents might have strong convictions about content and methods, and in particular that we might encounter a number of parents arguing forcibly for 'traditional' methods. But in fact, such parents were greatly outnumbered by those who had no clear views on the matter and who seemed happy to trust the teachers' professional judgement. Indeed, the most striking feature of this whole approach was the close agreement between the parents' responses when asked 'what should be taught?' and when asked 'what is being taught?' These points will be illustrated for each of the three core subjects.

Parents and English

In Year 1, well over half the parents thought that children should be learning the basic skills of reading and writing, and about a third of the parents spontaneously mentioned aspects of spoken language. Almost all these parents thought that these skills were already being taught:

> To learn to read, to express themselves in conversation.

> Speech, language – there's too much slang – writing, spelling and reading.

> Read, write, spell simple words, encourage to express themselves in a group. Listen and make up stories using imagination.

> Use the imagination, express herself, to listen to poetry, stories, to get thoughts down well, understand sentences.

Spelling was explicitly mentioned by just under a quarter of the parents as something which should be taught, although most of these parents felt it was being adequately covered in their child's school. There were a few parents, however, who expressed dissatisfactions in this area:

> They've got to learn to speak and write properly. For example, they're allowed to write 'throwed' when it should be 'threw'. I don't think that's correct. They've got to learn proper spelling, not just what it sounds like.

Only seven parents spontaneously mentioned a desire for more 'traditional methods', and this number was identical to those who wanted more emphasis on 'informal methods'. On the whole, the parents had relatively little to say about teaching methods, although there were the occasional advocates for different approaches. The following parent, for example, advocated an approach not too distant from the so-called 'real books' method:

> Reading's the most important thing. You've got to cultivate an interest in books. The writing will follow when you've got that.

In contrast, the next parent seemed to be suggesting an approach which was closer to the 'phonics' method:

They've got to start from the bottom and work up. Start with 'a', 'b', 'c' and then move on to words. From reading you go on to writing.

In Year 2, just under half the parents said they had found something 'surprising' in what or how their children were being taught in English. The most common source of surprise was that the methods used were different from what the parents had experienced themselves, or what they had encountered with older children. However, it would be wrong to equate surprise with criticism. While some parents were concerned about the methods used, and did not see why a particular approach was being taken, there were others who could see the advantages of an alternative approach:

I'm surprised that they started to do joined-up writing so young. It's younger than when I did it. Mind you, he loves it.

Where parents were critical of reading methods, they tended to express concern that their child was not being given enough individual attention in the classroom, or that the methods used were not suited to their particular child. In some cases parents felt they were having to compensate at home for inadequacies at school:

I've found it surprising that she is not catered for as an individual. She doesn't seem to have been assessed for individual needs, just pushed along as the group is pushed along. Her teacher's aware and does try, but there's just too many children and not enough time.

He can read harder than what he brings home. He's been on the same level book since he started. Maybe it's because they've got too many children – they can't hear them all individually. I think he can do better than they're allowing. They're not bringing out what he's got there.

I think the methods are wrong. He brings home fact books – he can't possibly learn to read from them. I buy him reading books.

Such concerns, it should be emphasized, were only expressed by a small minority of parents: most parents seemed happy with the methods used to teach their children to read and write. To say this is not to devalue these particular concerns, or to suggest that some children may indeed have been receiving inappropriate materials or inadequate individual attention. The point is simply that we did not unearth a major groundswell of discontent amongst parents with the content and methods used in teaching English.

Parents and maths

When asked in Year 1 what their children should be learning in maths, about half the parents mentioned basic number skills such as addition and subtraction, while around a fifth mentioned counting or multiplication tables. Virtually all these parents thought their children were currently being taught these things. Very few parents spontaneously said that they wanted a return to 'traditional methods', although one parent was quite explicit about this:

> I would like the old-fashioned way of teaching sums – sitting in rows.

Such parents were in fact outnumbered by those who spontaneously advocated more 'practical methods', or who emphasized that maths should be made interesting and enjoyable:

> They've got to learn the basics, sums. But they should also learn to enjoy numbers, that they're not something to worry about.

> They should be taught how to think about maths. Not by rote, but by playing with maths. They should make it fun and enjoyable.

In Year 2, about a third of the parents said they found some aspect of their children's maths 'surprising'. The most common source of surprise was that the methods and content of their children's maths learning were different from when the parents themselves were taught maths. As with English, this was not necessarily a criticism; indeed, several parents remarked on how advanced the work seemed or how much more interesting the modern methods were:

She's happy with maths. She's always getting us to give her sums and so on. There seems to be algebra involved – things we didn't do until secondary school.

I don't understand it as I didn't have the same system. They don't just do adding up and multiplying but things like counting the legs of insects. They use maths in wider aspects, the topics are very interrelated. I like this way of looking at education as a whole.

She was on the other day about co-ordinates and grids. It surprised me.

They do block graphs. It felt forward for her age. They use methods of learning tables not by rote like I did but by the 'brick-wall' method. They find the point in the middle. It's a good way of learning and helps with other things as well, not just tables. It makes it more interesting.

As with English, it seemed that the parents did not have any major dissatisfactions with what their children were doing in maths. While this may partly have been due to lack of knowledge, it was also clear from their responses that where they did know what was going on they were often well disposed towards it.

Parents and science

The parents' comments about science were of a different nature from their comments about English and maths. This was mainly because they were much less knowledgeable about science than they were about the other two core subjects: they knew less about what their children were actually doing in science, and they had fewer ideas about what their children should be doing. Nevertheless, there were still a number of parents who ventured an opinion on what their children should be taught. Their suggestions came under headings such as 'basic scientific concepts', 'how things work', 'nature study', 'properties of materials', 'the environment' and 'simple experiments', although they were often not expressed in precisely those terms:

To understand why certain things happen.

Basic concepts. General principles, working things out. The fact that they're doing anything is great. We live in a technological age.

Natural science, the world around them. Domestic science, recipes, cooking. Simple experiments.

How water behaves, floating and sinking, absorption, magnets. It's got to be very practical at this age.

General awareness of his environment and the world around him. He's interested in how things work. He's encouraged in this line.

The differences between substances, temperature, materials, uses for materials, what things are made of. Their curiosity is endless at this age.

As with English and maths, we did not unearth any great discrepancy between what the parents thought should be taught and what they thought actually was taught. Indeed, the proportion of parents saying they found anything 'surprising' in Year 2 was lower for science than for either of the other two core subjects. Moreover, it was clear from their responses to this question – as well as from some of the quotes above – that many parents were not only pleased with the fact that science was being taught but were impressed by the positive effect it was having on their child. 'All made so interesting', 'amazed at what they cover' and 'surprised at the questions they ask' were the three most frequently mentioned sources of surprise in science:

Yes, it all sinks in. They went out and named trees. Before he was just a plodder, now he really takes an interest. The teacher's good and makes an effort, she's very organized. My son isn't bored any more.

It amazed me that her eating changed (as a result of school science). We now have discussions every mealtime, about things like how much food is taken. She asks 'what is danger food?' and thinks that anything with sugar is a danger. Her attitude to sweets has changed.

> She wants to be involved in everything we do at home. I didn't think she would be. Her questions are surprising. Mashed potato came into it somewhere – she asked 'how do you get mashed potato?' the other day.

> He loves science. He asked the other night 'how far does the sky go on for?' and 'how far does space go on for?'

These comments suggest that the increased emphasis on science at Key Stage One has been well received by parents. As we saw earlier in the chapter, several parents who were initially uncertain about the nature or value of science for children at this age became more positive – and even enthusiastic – towards it as the study progressed. A critical factor for these parents was the obvious interest and enjoyment being expressed by their children at home about the science they were experiencing at school.

Parents and the foundation subjects

At the time of the Year 1 interviews the programmes of study for the various foundation subjects (history, geography, technology, art, music and PE) had not yet been formally introduced. Nevertheless, most of the schools in our study were already doing something in these areas. We were interested in whether the parents approved of these subjects being part of the curriculum at this age. As we did not expect the parents to know what the foundation subjects were, we gave them this information as part of the Year 1 interview: we then asked if they thought it was a good idea for these subjects to be introduced into the curriculum for children aged 5–7 years.

The majority of parents were in favour of the foundation subjects being introduced (see figure 7.3). Most parents simply indicated their approval, but some gave a more detailed explanation of why each subject was important. The following parent, for example, went through the list of foundation subjects and gave an explicit reason of why each subject (apart from technology) earned its place in the curriculum:

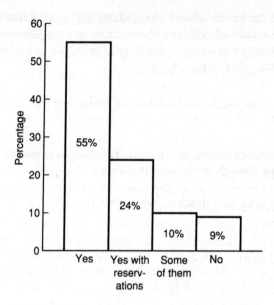

Figure 7.3 Do parents approve of the foundation subjects being introduced? (Year 1, $n = 138$.)

> I would have thought so in this day and age. History's important. Geography is important too because of different countries in the class – different creeds, colours, religions. Art gives you an appreciation of other things. PE gets rid of aggression. And music's relaxing.

The next parent also approved of the foundation subjects, but did not offer any justifications as to why particular subjects might be introduced. Instead, she felt it should be left to the children to decide what should or should not be in the curriculum:

> Give them a chance, and if they like it stick to it. Give the National Curriculum a chance, and give the children a chance to approve or disapprove.

A number of parents approved of the foundation subjects in principle but expressed qualifications or reservations about their introduction. These reservations took two main forms. First, there were some concerns about the practicalities of fitting all these subjects into the school day. Some parents questioned whether there was enough time, or proper resources, or whether it might be too confusing for the children:

> A taste of as much as possible. It comes down to time and resources.

> I've reservations about the number. It's a lot to concentrate on at 5. It's hard enough with just one subject.

> You can't cram too much in when they're young. It might cause confusion.

Other parents were more concerned about how the subjects were introduced. Many remembered how they had been taught these subjects in formal lessons in secondary school, and not surprisingly considered that this was inappropriate for younger children:

> I don't think at this age they should be learning as subjects, but rather through the medium of other subjects. For example, they did something on the local topography in English.

> In a small way, yes. But I wonder whether 5–6 year olds can cope with it. It depends how they're approached.

A few parents were definitely opposed to introducing the foundation subjects at this age. This was usually because they felt it would take attention away from more essential things:

> I wouldn't have thought they could take it all in at that age. The basics could suffer.

> Very basically, English, maths and science are the most important at an early age. The others can be introduced in detail later.

Despite these reservations, it was clear that most parents supported in principle the idea that young children should be taught a wide range of subjects. While no parent actually used the phrase

Parents and the National Curriculum　145

which is often associated with the National Curriculum – that it should be a 'broad and balanced curriculum' – there was little doubt that the idea would have met with general approval.

The parents were also asked each year whether any of the foundation subjects were already being taught to their children. This question produced a distinct split between art, music and PE on the one hand, and history, geography and technology on the other. Almost all the parents thought that their children were encountering the first group of subjects throughout this period. This was partly because these subjects were more familiar to the parents, being a long-established part of the infant school curriculum. But it was also because they were frequently confronted with direct evidence that they were doing these subjects – in the form of paintings brought home from school or dirty PE kit to be washed:

He brings home drawings on scrappy bits of paper.

They don't bring paintings home any more but I can tell they've done art by the mess of them.

He is always coming home singing.

They do more music now. A good idea too, it gives more balance. Not that I want a budding rock star, although they can if it makes more money – anything's better than farming.

They go swimming once a fortnight. They play five-a-side football with other schools. I go and watch.

They do a bit (of PE) and they need it. There's a real lack of health in her classmates.

Parents were much less certain whether their children had encountered the other three foundation subjects – technology, geography and history. This was partly because, as we have already seen, many parents simply did not know enough about what their children were doing on a day-to-day basis in the classroom. But it was also because many parents were unsure exactly what these subjects looked like for children aged 5–7 years. Indeed, parents frequently responded to questions about technology, history or

geography by trying to think of something their child had recently done which might conceivably count as one of these subjects:

> I don't think he's done much technology at all – unless you include
> cooking.

> Well, they're always cutting things out – making boxes. Is that
> technology?

> From the things he says they must do geography now. All this
> business with the ozone thing. They talk about different countries.

> He did ask if somewhere was in England or was it in Southtown?
> But I didn't associate that with geography.

> They do a lot about Jesus – is that history?

> They're always on about the Romans.

These comments make clear that while parents were on slightly
surer ground with the three more traditional areas of art, music
and PE, their ideas about the newer foundation subjects of technology, history and geography were frequently characterized by
uncertainty and confusion. The comments also raise the more
general issues of what parents know about what their children are
doing in school, and how they obtain this knowledge. We will
explore these issues more fully in the next chapter.

Overview

When the National Curriculum was introduced, it was assumed
it would be widely welcomed by parents. It would give them,
possibly for the first time ever, detailed information about what
their children were doing at school and about how they were
getting on. It was also thought that parents would welcome the
emphasis on basics which was implied by putting English, maths
and science at the core of the curriculum, as well as appreciating
the 'broad and balanced' curriculum provided by the foundation
subjects.

We found only partial support for these assumptions. While the majority of parents were in favour of the National Curriculum, many raised concerns about it, both in principle and in practice. Similarly, while the majority of parents were in favour of having English, maths and science at the core, many felt this focus on the basics was too limited. And while the majority of parents were in favour of introducing the foundation subjects at this age, concerns were also raised about the desirability and practicality of doing this.

We found little support for the frequently voiced belief that most parents want a return to traditional methods. Asking parents what should be taught in three core subjects, and how that teaching should take place, generated few demands for a return to traditional methods: indeed, parents were more likely to advocate practical approaches to learning, or to say that learning should be interesting – or even fun – than they were to propose a return to traditional methods.

Finally, we pointed out on more than one occasion in this chapter that the parents did not seem to know very much about what their children were learning in school. This is clearly an important issue, given that one of the main arguments for the National Curriculum is that it would make parents better informed about what their children were doing in the classroom. We will explore this issue more fully in the next chapter.

8

Parents' Knowledge about School

I know nothing. Yes, I would like to know more. But I
don't want to be lectured on it – just a handout.
(Parent's comment on information about Key Stage Two)

One theme which persistently emerges from previous research
on parents is that they do not feel sufficiently well informed about
what is happening in their children's schools. Thus Becher, Eraut
and Knight (1981) talk about parents' 'great thirst for information about what their children are doing at school', while Munn
(1985) argues that parents want 'more direct and specific information about what their child is doing at school and how he is
progressing'. In the same vein, a review of research on parents'
views in the period 1985–90 by MacBeath and Weir (1991)
concludes that 'one of the main sources of criticism from parents
is lack of information'. MacBeath and Weir also note that parents
are frequently reliant on their children as the main source of
information about the school, that parents find school reports
inadequate and want more personalized information and advice,
and that parents find it difficult to appraise their children's progress
because they are unsure what standards are expected of them.
  It is not surprising, in view of the above, that many parents in
our study thought that one of the main benefits of the National
Curriculum would be that they would know more about what
and how their children were doing at school (see chapter 7). They

would certainly have been supported in this belief by much of the official literature about the current reforms which has been produced for parents. For example, a pamphlet entitled 'Your Child and the National Curriculum', produced by the Department of Education and Science in 1991, contained a foreword by Kenneth Clarke, then Secretary of State for Education. Clarke wrote as follows:

> Your child has a right to a good education, and you have a right to know both what is being taught in your child's school and how your child is progressing. That is why we now have a National Curriculum which sets out for the first time what children should know, understand and be able to do at each stage of their education from 5 to 16.

The idea that parents want to know more about what is happening in school was evidently not shared by the headteachers who took part in our telephone survey (see chapter 2). Most of the heads felt that their parents were generally uninformed about the National Curriculum and assessment, and, more strikingly, that they did not want to know anything more about these topics. Parents were frequently described as having little interest in what went on at school, as long as their children seemed happy. Indeed, many headteachers were more concerned with how they could generate interest amongst seemingly apathetic parents than in how they could satisfy any great parental thirst for information.

In this chapter we will examine these issues from the perspective of the parents in our study. We focus on the following questions:

- How much did parents know about the National Curriculum and assessment? Did they want to know more about these topics?
- Did parents feel they knew enough about what their children were doing in English, maths and science?
- How much did parents know about Key Stage Two (7–11 years)?
- What kind of contacts did parents have with the school? What kind of information was provided by these contacts?

Parents' knowledge about the National Curriculum

At the time of the Year 1 interviews the National Curriculum had only just been introduced. Not surprisingly, the parents' knowledge about it in these first interviews was not very extensive. Almost all the parents knew about its existence, and around three-quarters knew that English, maths and science made up the core subjects, but beyond that their knowledge was limited. Their main source of information was the school – either from parents' evenings or from literature sent home – although some parents mentioned they had heard about the National Curriculum from the media or from other sources. The few parents who claimed they had not heard of the National Curriculum came mostly from one school which at the time of the first interviews had done very little to inform its parents about what was going on.

The great majority of parents (83 per cent) said in the Year 1 interviews that they would like to know more about the National Curriculum. Typically, they wanted to have more details about what their children would be doing in each subject at each age level. This point was expressed particularly clearly by the following parent, who contrasted her current knowledge of what her children should be doing with the knowledge she had had when they were younger:

> I want to know what is expected of 6- and 7-year-olds. When they were babies I knew what they were supposed to be doing, but I don't know now they're at school.

The parents' interest in the National Curriculum was not simply confined to their own children. Some parents wanted to know more about its wider effects on the school as a whole, while others wanted greater understanding about its nature and purpose. The following quotes give some idea of the range of the parents' desire for further information:

How it's going to affect this school.

How it's going to be put into practice. What resources are going to be made available.

The percentage given to each subject. They cancelled the Christmas play because of the National Curriculum – I want to know why that was necessary.

Why it's so different from now. Whether they will they be doing project work. What happens at certain ages.

More about the background. Why it came about. What are its actual aims – in a sentence, succinct. Does it apply to private schools?

and finally, the rather plaintive

Lots of things, so I can understand.

Most of the parents thought this information should come from the school, although some thought it should come from local or national authorities, preferably in the form of an easy-to-read booklet. One parent, however, could see disadvantages to both these sources:

Teachers have enough on their plates, and I can't understand the documents, so I'm not sure where the information should come from!

While the great majority of parents wanted more information about the National Curriculum, there was a small minority (16 per cent) who said they did not want to know any more about it. Over half these parents felt they already knew enough, while the others produced a mixture of reasons. Some felt that it would be some time before the National Curriculum was fully implemented, or pointed out that large parts of it had not yet been decided on. Others felt that information was of little use as they had no power to change things. Finally, there were a few parents who felt that the time and money spent on informing parents would be better spent on their children's education.

In the Year 2 interviews, those parents who had said in Year 1 that they wanted to know more about the National Curriculum were asked whether they now felt they knew more about it. Despite their evident desire for more information the previous year, only half of these parents (52 per cent) felt they were any more knowledgeable one year later. Moreover, many of these parents qualified their replies by saying that they were only 'a bit' more knowledgeable, or that they 'thought' they knew more. Mostly their knowledge had come from the school, although some commented that it had come from other sources, such as the media or their children. As the following examples show, parents had different opinions on whether this new information had been helpful:

> Yes. I'm not aware of in-depth details like specific attainment targets, but enough to feel happy.

> Yes, slightly more, through asking the children what they're doing at school. How they're doing lots more science and project work. Also by talking to the other mums. Nothing has come home from the school.

> Yes and no. I bought *The National Curriculum: A Survival Guide* from the bookshop and it's been some help. Going in to help in the classroom has been useful too. I've looked at some of the literature on technology, I've looked at the targets. But I've just become more confused.

Just under half the parents (48 per cent) said they were no more knowledgeable in Year 2 than they had been a year previously. Most of these parents said they had heard nothing from the school during this period. While some parents were critical of the school for not keeping them informed, others more sympathetically pointed out that the teachers had enough to do keeping themselves informed. Some parents also mentioned that there had been meetings at the school which might have provided more information but which they had been unable to attend. A few parents had tried to find out from other sources, but had not experienced much success:

Not really, I've not been given any more information. You could look at the books but they're so detailed they put you off. I've not actually been given anything about it.

Still foggy. I've had a leaflet from the school, but no one has gone into details except when it first started. I think teachers are trying to keep on top of it themselves, let alone telling us.

I saw a book in Smiths but thought 'why should I buy it?' It should come from the school, but it hasn't.

It is clear from these comments that whilst something had been done between Years 1 and 2 to satisfy parents' desire for more information, it was not enough. Despite the fact that their children were in the first year of one of the most important educational innovations ever seen, the great majority of parents were still very much in the dark about what was going on. Moreover, it did not seem at all clear as to whose responsibility it was – the school, local or national authorities, or the parents themselves – to ensure that parents were kept adequately informed.

Parents' knowledge about the core subjects

In the Year 3 interviews we felt it was no longer appropriate to ask parents about their knowledge of the National Curriculum in general, and focused instead on the three core subjects of English, maths and science. We pointed out that their child had now completed Key Stage One of the National Curriculum, and asked how much they felt they knew about what had been taught in these subjects during that period. The parents were specifically asked whether they felt they had 'a lot of knowledge', 'some knowledge' or 'little or no knowledge' of what their child had been taught. They were also asked if they would have liked to have known more about these subjects.

The majority of parents did not feel very knowledgeable about what their children had been taught in the three core subjects (see table 8.1). Most parents considered that they either had 'some

Table 8.1 How much did parents feel they knew about the core subjects? (Year 3, *n* = 124.)

	English	Maths	Science
A lot of knowledge	18%	29%	19%
Some knowledge	41%	36%	27%
Little or no knowledge	41%	35%	54%

knowledge' or 'little or no knowledge' about what their children had been learning. There was some variation from subject to subject, in that parents were most likely to say they had 'little or no knowledge' about science, and most likely to say they had 'a lot of knowledge' about maths. Nevertheless, the overall picture is that the parents did not feel well informed about these three central areas of the curriculum.

While the parents were not specifically asked where their knowledge had come from, their spontaneous comments were quite revealing. For English and maths, their main sources of information were from direct contact with the school (such as attending parents' evenings, looking at work in the classroom, or talking to the teacher), from work that the child brought home from school, or from work which the child actually carried out at home. The picture for science was rather different, in that parents were much less likely to mention these sources and much more likely to say that their knowledge had come from what their child spontaneously told them about what they had been doing at school. Indeed, many parents commented that their children talked more about science than about any other subject.

More than half the parents would have liked to know more about what their children were doing in the three core subjects (see table 8.2). Typically, parents said they would have liked more detailed knowledge about what the children were doing on a day-to-day basis, although some also mentioned that they would have appreciated knowing more about what was required for the assessments. Many parents pointed out that it was difficult extracting this information from their children, particularly if they were tired at the end of a long day, and that a short information

Table 8.2 Would parents have liked to know more? (Year 3, *n* = 124.)

	English	Maths	Science
Yes	55%	52%	58%
No	43%	46%	40%

sheet explaining what was going to be covered in the next few weeks would have been extremely useful:

English I'd like to know more about the sorts of things they do in class. English is so general, it's difficult to tell what they're doing. Children can't say or define what they're doing, as they can in maths. It's difficult to tell what stage they're at.

It wouldn't be too difficult at the beginning of the year to be sent a breakdown of areas of work to be covered. It wouldn't be very expensive or time consuming either.

Maths How he was getting on with sums and times-tables. What he's doing on them.

Exactly how they're working things out these days. It's so different, that if I wanted to help I can't.

Science I don't know what's classified as science. She talks about things done which I presume are science, but I'd like to know in a more specific way.

It still remains a mystery to me – and to the children, I suspect. I don't think they know they are doing science. I would have liked to have known specifically what was science. I could have got books from the library about science topics.

Nearly half the parents said they did not want to know more about what their children had been doing in these subjects (see table 8.2). Most of these parents felt they already knew 'a lot' about what had been taught in each subject and that further information was unnecessary. However, there was a small group of parents who claimed to have 'little or no knowledge' about what their children were doing, but who still said they did not want to know more. Typically, these parents justified their position by saying that their child had no problems, that they trusted the teachers, or that they could always ask the school if they wanted to know more.

Parents' knowledge about assessment

During the Year 1 interviews the parents were asked how much they knew about the standardized assessments which their children were due to undertake some 18 months later. At the time of these interviews there was still a great deal of official confusion and uncertainty about what the assessments would actually consist of. It was known that some sort of assessment would be carried out, and that it would focus on the three core subjects of English, maths and science; however, it was not yet clear how far the assessment would be based on teachers' own judgements about children, and how far it would involve the use of standardized tests. There was also a great deal of uncertainty about how and to whom the results would subsequently be reported. Official documents at the time suggested that the results would not be reported to parents, and that league tables of local education authorities would not be drawn up and made public – although both these positions were subsequently reversed.

In view of this offical confusion and uncertainty, it is not surprising that the parents' knowledge about assessment at the time of the Year 1 interviews was somewhat hazy. Three-quarters of the parents knew that children were to be assessed as part of the new National Curriculum, and just over half the parents were aware that their own child would be assessed in 1991. However, the majority of parents were unclear what form this assessment would take. Some thought that it would be done by teachers' own assessments, some by exam-like tests, and some had simply no idea. The parents were also unclear about the reporting arrangements. Over half the parents did not know whether they would be told their child's results, although almost all of them thought that they should be given this information: typically, they commented that it would enable them to give their children extra help in weak areas.

Virtually all the parents (98 per cent) said they wanted to know more about assessment. As with information about the National Curriculum, most of the parents thought this information should be provided by the school. They wanted to know why the assessment was being undertaken, how it would be carried out, what it would involve for their children and what their role as parents would be. Some of their comments indicated they had underlying concerns about assessment and that some degree of reassurance would be welcome:

> I want to know what they're aiming at with this assessment. What's the reason behind it all?

> How do they plan to do it? Some children find exams difficult and some don't.

> How, who with? I hope there's not any pressure.

> I want to be told exactly what they're going to be tested on, and whether it's the same for everyone.

> I want to know whether it's going to be recorded for ever. I'm worried about labelling children as 'successes' or 'failures'.

By the time of the Year 2 interviews the situation had become somewhat clearer. The assessments were due to start in a few months time, and it was known that they would be a combination of teacher assessment (TA) and standard assessment tasks (SATs); it was also known that the results of the assessments would be reported to parents. However, the parents themselves did not appear to be much more knowledgeable, despite the virtually unanimous desire for more information which they had expressed the previous year. Nearly three-quarters (72 per cent) of the parents felt they did not know any more about assessment than they did in Year 1, with the main comment being that they had heard nothing more from the school. As with information about the National Curriculum, many parents seemed unclear as to whose responsibility it should be to keep them informed.

> I don't really know any more than I did before. I'm not sure where the information is available. I've been given none.

> We've got a lot of concerns. Nobody could tell us what form the assessments would take, or how the children would cope. The teachers didn't even know.

> I don't know what they expect a child to do at 7. There's been no information from the school – but there again, I haven't asked. But perhaps I shouldn't have to ask. It's handy to know what a child can do.

The limitations in the parents' knowledge were revealed by their answers to other questions. Less than a third of the parents knew what subjects their child would be assessed in, and only a fifth knew that the results would be reported to them. Less than a quarter had any idea of how the assessments would be carried out, although a similar proportion had heard of the term 'SAT'. Indeed, it seemed that little had been done to reduce the confusion and uncertainty seen in the previous year's interviews, or to alleviate parents' concerns. Their children were about to take part in the first ever assessment of 7-year-olds, and yet the parents seemed to have little idea of what was going to take place. We will return to this issue in chapter 9, when we look more closely at what actually happened during and after the assessments themselves.

Parents' knowledge about Key Stage Two

At the time of the final interview, the children were approaching the end of their first term in Key Stage Two (7–11 years). It therefore seemed appropriate to ask the parents how much they knew about this phase of their children's schooling, and whether they would like to know more about it.

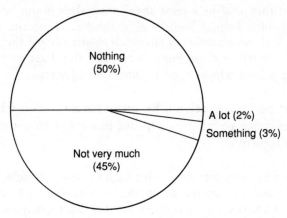

Figure 8.1 How much did parents know about Key Stage Two? (Year 3, *n* = 124.)

The parents' knowledge about Key Stage Two appeared to be minimal. As figure 8.1 shows, virtually all the parents said they knew 'not very much' or 'nothing' about this stage. Many pointed out that they had received little information from the school on what would be happening to their child during this period. Some parents had strong feelings on the matter:

> I know nothing. I've had nothing from the school. I feel the school is letting us down.

Almost all the parents (96 per cent) said they would like to know more about Key Stage Two, and most of these parents felt this information should come from the school. As with Key Stage One, the parents typically wanted to know what their children would be taught in each subject at each level, with many pointing out that this information would enable them to help their children more effectively at home. A particular interest was shown in what new subjects would be introduced, with a large number of parents hoping their children would start a foreign language at this stage:

> I'd like to know if she's going to do a language. But also just generally more on what she's covering, but not too far ahead.

Maybe if they told us a term ahead what she's going to do and how we could help at home – although I can't see the teachers doing that as some parents might coach children or put them under pressure. Or tell us about things we could offer. I get no feedback from the school when I send in things for projects.

This last point was echoed by other parents, who felt that the school was quick to ask for help but less ready to provide information in return:

I'd like to know more about what he'll be doing. It helps if you, the child and the school are working in conjunction with one another. They don't let you know yet they ask for helpers. I don't know if that's right – it's not professional.

One parent made it particularly clear how she would like to receive her information:

I know nothing. Yes, I would like to know more. But I don't want to be lectured on it – just a handout.

Not all the parents were dissatisfied with the amount of information they were getting. Some teachers were evidently making a particular effort to communicate with parents about what the children were doing in school, and when this happened it was greatly appreciated:

The teacher explained what they're doing in the year to come in history, geography and science. She went through the whole thing and explained the topics for the year. I expect we'll learn more as we go along. I'm happy at the moment.

The parents' comments about Key Stage Two are very similar to the ones reported earlier about Key Stage One. Their children were entering a new stage of the National Curriculum, one which might have important consequences for the rest of their formal education, yet the parents were left feeling very much in the dark about what would be happening to them. More disturbingly, there seemed to be a growing sense of bitterness behind some of the parents' comments – as if they were becoming increasingly frustrated by their lack of knowledge about what was happening to their children in school.

Parents' contact with the school

In order to throw more light on the methods by which parents were – or were not – obtaining information about their child's school, we asked them during the Year 2 interviews about their contact with the school during the previous 12 months. We enquired specifically about a number of different types of contact, such as receiving newsletters or attending meetings, and tried to find out what information had been transmitted or received through each type of contact.

There had clearly been extensive contact between the parents and the schools during the previous 12 months (see figure 8.2). The most common means of communication was the newsletter: every parent had received at least one newsletter during the year,

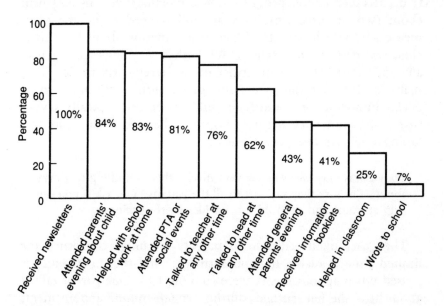

Figure 8.2 Parents' contact with the school (Year 2, *n* = 122).

and most parents had received several. These newsletters typically contained general information about what was happening at the school, such as dates of forthcoming events or outings, items of Parent Teacher Association (PTA) or governor business, or news about staff changes. Newsletters also contained frequent requests for help, but little information about the curriculum. While they seemed to be generally appreciated, some parents expressed concern about the unreliability of the newsletter as a means of communication: they reported missing events because they had not been informed, and were left wondering whether the newsletter had got lost on the way home or whether it had never existed in the first place. Some parents also expressed irritation about the large numbers of requests for help which could not always be responded to:

> They pester us. They're forever asking us to do things. When I was working I couldn't. They asked us to paint classrooms – there is a limit!

The great majority of parents had attended a parents' evening to discuss their child's progress. These meetings were usually held about two or three times a year, and seemed to be the main method by which parents obtained information about how their child was getting on at school. While these evenings were generally appreciated, two main criticisms were regularly made. First, many parents felt they were not given sufficiently accurate or detailed information about their child's progress, typically saying that it was not very helpful simply to be told their child was 'doing fine'. As one parent put it:

> They always say 'she's doing very nicely, there's nothing to worry about'. I'm sure they say that to all the parents. You ask if you can help at home and get told no. I'd like more specifics.

The other main criticism of parents' evenings concerned the limited time available for appointments, and the inconvenience caused when appointments were running late. One parent talked about how she felt 'rushed' during her ten-minute appointment, and that she forgot all the things she was wanting to ask about:

she added that she would try to write them down next time. Another parent was particularly annoyed by her experience:

> I had an appointment, but I had to sit waiting for three-quarters of an hour. Another mother was in with the teacher all the time. I had to sit and watch a video of the children on a camping trip instead. I couldn't stay down there for ever, as I had a chicken on. I went home without seeing the teacher.

The other main way in which parents obtained information about their child's progress was by discussing this informally with the teacher. Many parents appreciated the willingness with which teachers were prepared to make themselves available for short conversations during the working day, and often these conversations seemed to be enough to put parents' minds at rest over a particular problem. As one parent put it:

> They're always welcoming, never off-putting. I can't imagine my mother going into my classroom to talk to the teacher. It must be a change for the better.

About a quarter of the parents said they had not talked to the teacher outside of parents' evenings at any time during the previous year. There appeared to be several reasons for this. In some cases, the parent being interviewed did not or could not take their child to or from school, leaving this to the other parent or a friend, while in other cases the parent simply dropped or collected the child at the school gate and did not go into the school or classroom. There were also a number of parents who said that they found it hard to approach the school staff: they talked about not wanting to 'pester' the teachers, or feeling that they were 'too busy' to be approached. One parent commented:

> I do feel you have to have a reason to ask. You can't help feeling the teacher's got better things to do.

Another parent expressed it more starkly:

> I only go in if I'm desperate!

As figure 8.2 shows, the other main forms of contact mentioned by parents were helping with schoolwork at home (usually listening to their child read), attending PTA or social events, and talking informally to the teacher or headteacher. Parents were less likely to have attended a general parents' evening (often because they were held at inconvenient times), received an information booklet or helped out in the classroom. Very few parents had written to the head on any matter.

The majority of parents (67 per cent) said they did not want to have any more contact with the school than they already did. Many parents pointed out that they had other commitments, such as work or younger children to look after, while several made comments along the lines of 'it's there if you want it'. Other parents suggested that there was some form of barrier between parents and teachers which was likely to limit the value of such contact:

We feel we should do more, but they also regard it as us and them.

I only want more contact if the school is willing to take on what you say.

This last point was made more extensively by the following parent. She described how in her younger child's class the teacher kept a folder of each child's work and parents were asked to make comments. She went on to say:

It's good if they use it. Home life can affect how they learn and how they fit in with others. But they do need to use it if they ask for it. If they want you to work with them, they have to work with you. If they ask you for information they should use it. They keep telling you they're individuals but this doesn't tally with their actions.

The evidence presented here suggests that most parents had a considerable amount of contact – both formal and informal – with their child's school. Nevertheless, we were left feeling that this contact was frequently failing to provide parents with the type of communication which they really wanted. While parents were quick to praise teachers who were open and welcoming, there was still a pervasive feeling of inhibition on the parents' part about approaching the school, either to obtain information or to discuss a particular problem. Moreover, it may be this kind of inhibition on the parents' part – or the desire not to 'pester' hard-working teachers – which the headteachers in our telephone survey interpreted as 'disinterest' or 'apathy'.

The parents' diaries

In order to learn more about the communication taking place between home and school, we asked the parents in Year 2 if they would complete a diary describing all their contacts with the school over a 2-week period. The diary took the form of a small booklet with spaces for each day. On one side of the page the parents were asked for information about the type of contact they had had with the school, while on the other side they were asked to give details of what the contact had been about.

Virtually all the parents agreed to complete the diary and return it to us in a stamped addressed envelope, although in the end only 76 diaries (59 per cent of the sample) were actually received. The timing of the Year 2 interviews (late in the autumn term) meant that many of these contacts concerned Christmas, thus providing a degree of seasonal bias to our findings. Nevertheless, the completed diaries still provide a fascinating insight into the nature and content of the communication taking place between home and school (figure 8.3).

The diaries provided further evidence of a large and varied amount of formal and informal contact between parents and schools. The most frequently mentioned contact was hearing about things from their children, followed by receiving newsletters, going into the school/classroom and seeing things for themselves, and talking to the teacher. Other less common forms of contact were phone calls to or from the school (usually about the child being ill), talking to the headteacher, attending evening meetings such as the annual parent/governor meeting or curriculum events, speaking to non-teaching staff and conversations with other parents. More seasonal activities included going to school to see the Christmas play, attending church for the school Carol Service,

Date: 18·12·90	TYPE OF CONTACT	About
No contact with teacher		about the moon and their space project at school – he told me what a crescent moon was.
John talked		No mention of the school party!

Date: 19·12·90		
Chat with Headmistress		Very informal – asked about my new job & how my back was fairing! John wasn't mentioned I'm afraid!
John talked		He thought his spelling was good today!

Date: 19·12·90		
No contact with teacher		He'd made candles in class & told me about the wick being flattened & the candle being a 'funny shape' (a hemisphere but he'd forgotten the word!)
John talked		

Figure 8.3 A typical page from the parents' diaries.

taking in contributions for the children's Christmas party or helping out in the grotto.

Visits to the classroom were often made at the instigation of the child, who wanted to show their parent something they had done or made: such visits usually took place at the beginning or end of the school day. Other parents mentioned helping the teacher by listening to children reading, watching over a maths test, making a Christmas cake, making a collage and helping with swimming. There were two instances of what might be called parent education. In one case the school held reading workshops where parents came in to read with their own child at the end of the day: as part of this programme the school had shown a video about the teaching of reading and followed this with a discussion. The other instance was where a parent attended a French class held for parents at the school: this parent wanted to be able to help her children when they started to learn French.

Talking to the teacher was another common form of contact, and these conversations covered a wide variety of topics. Some parents used this opportunity to discuss their child's progress, while others discussed their child's social abilities or their attitude to work. Reading was frequently mentioned, particularly in the context of choosing books to bring home. There were a few isolated discussions of particular classroom activities and the rationale behind them. One child told his mother that the teacher had brought in a telescope but had not yet used it. The mother asked the teacher if they were going to use it and for what purpose. The teacher replied that the project was 'Round and Round, Off and Away' (followed by exclamation marks in the parent's diary) and that they would be studying the moon, earth, planets, universe and so on. The teacher also explained that although there was not much that could be done with the telescope, they would look through different lenses including an inverting one (again followed by exclamation marks in the diary).

Another common reason for talking to the teacher was to pass on personal information about the child. Sometimes this was to say that the child had not been well, or that there were difficulties of some kind at home. In one case the child had a new baby half-sister (born to his father's new partner), and his mother was concerned about her son's reaction to this event. There were also many conversations about lost property, typically about clothes that had been lost at school and which the parent was hoping would turn up, or about school books that had been lost at home. Sometimes such conversations would stretch over several days, ending happily with 'the . . . has now been found!'. Several parents evidently took an interest in the teacher's welfare, and asked how they were coping or if they had enjoyed a course they had attended.

Most parents received at least one newsletter from the school during the fortnight in which they kept the diary. These newsletters covered a wide variety of topics: in one school alone the parents received information about a Christmas fun evening and lottery, details of a toy and book sale, an order form for school sweat-shirts and T-shirts, news about a fund-raising coffee afternoon with cakes made by parents, and requests for support with the Christmas party. Other newsletters included information about change of school times, about staff leaving (in both cases not to be replaced), about charity fund-raising efforts, and about the annual parent/governor meeting. However, these newsletters contained little information about what the children were actually learning in the classroom.

Two schools organized curriculum meetings on the subject of reading, and both received comments from parents that they were well worth attending and much appreciated. Interestingly, two parents at one school gave different accounts of the same meeting. One parent saw it as the school counteracting reports in the national press of falling standards by explaining their own approach to the teaching of reading, while the other parent saw it as the school encouraging parents to become more involved in their children's reading, as the school was concerned about its own standards.

The most striking feature of the diaries was undoubtedly the *central role which the children were playing* in communication between home and school. It was clear that the children constituted the main means – and in many cases the only means – by which parents found out what went on at school. Thus we learnt from the diaries that in the area of maths, for example, the children had covered the size of dinosaurs, semi-circles, octagons, matching shapes, and pyramids; played computer tables games and completed sum cards; filled different containers with liquid; taken in a sixpence piece as it was a showing day; had problems with their maths card which the parent had to sort out with the teacher; made graphs of how many boys and how many girls there were in the class; 'done two pages of maths which he had done a long time ago but it was unfair because he had forgotten how to do them without using cubes'; measured everyone's feet; found addresses using co-ordinates and drawn around shadows on the playground. They were doing projects on space, water, dinosaurs, colour and light, shiny things, heat and 'experiments to see how salt melts ice and what happens when you put a wax crayon into hot water'. They had tried to find out if plasticine melted and made skeletons of diplodocus out of straws. They had practised endlessly for school plays and made Christmas cards, presents and wrapping paper. They had discussed time-machines going forwards and backwards and been 'fascinated by the sun, moon and stars'. They had then come home and told their parents all about it.

Sometimes the children wanted to continue or repeat at home

what they had done at school. They read from their reading books, but also looked for the Milky Way in the sky when it got dark. One child wanted to write a story about a dinosaur with a game in it: she took it back into school the next day and played it with her friends. Another child repeated the experiment with the ice and salt to show his mother that it worked, while a third finished her map of a treasure island and put in 'references' (co-ordinates).

The children also told their parents about how the teacher was ill and how they had a new teacher (whom they did or did not like); how somebody's father had come to talk about electricity; how the student had put them with partners whom they had to ask for spellings before asking him; how they wanted to take in boxes for models, socks for the Christmas picture and clean cans to make gas masks; how they had moved from red to blue reading books and had won two team points for their maths; how they were the leader of their group and had to organize the others; how they could not bring home a book unless they had done two pages of maths, and how they could bring home their owl collage because they had done 'good writing about fireworks today'.

Clearly, the children were providing parents with a fascinating wealth of information about what they were doing in school. But it is not immediately obvious what, if anything, the parents made of all this information. There is little evidence from the diaries that parents used what their children told them to initiate discussions with the teacher about what their children were doing or why they were doing it. In addition, much of the information provided by the children was fragmented and incomplete. Parents were being given glimpses into what their children were doing, but very little insight into why they were doing it or how it fitted into some larger scheme of things.

The picture emerging from these parent diaries fits closely with that provided earlier by our interviews. Both sources of evidence suggest that there is indeed a large and varied amount of contact between parents and schools. However, the communication which takes place across this contact is often of a fairly limited nature. Much of it is concerned with the practical side of school life, such as requesting help or other types of contribution, providing information about meetings, or discussing lost clothing. If parents want information about the curriculum, then they probably have to rely on their child as informant, while if they want information about progress, they must rely on the occasional parents' evening. In other words, it seems that parents and schools only rarely engage in direct communication about matters of central educational importance.

Overview

In this chapter we have looked at parents' knowledge about what is happening in their children's schools. We have looked at their knowledge of the National Curriculum and assessment, at their knowledge of what their children are learning in the core subjects of English, maths and science, and at their knowledge of what will happen in Key Stage Two. We have also looked at the kinds of contact parents have with their child's school, and at the type of information being communicated by these contacts. Three main findings have emerged.

First, it is clear that the great majority of parents know very little about what is happening in their children's schools. In each of the areas examined, the parents in our study felt they knew little or nothing about what was going on. Moreover, the National Curriculum appears to have made little difference in this respect, despite the claims made by its advocates: our findings are remarkably similar to those obtained before the National Curriculum was introduced. Our findings have also raised the question of who is responsible for making sure parents are adequately informed – schools, local or national authorities, or parents themselves?

Second, while parents' knowledge in these areas was severely limited, their desire for more information was not. Each time parents were asked if they wanted to know more, the great majority replied that they did. Typically, they wanted to find out more about what their children were doing at school so they could provide more effective help for them at home. These findings might come as a surprise to many of the headteachers in our telephone survey, who felt that most of their parents had little interest in what went on at school. There seems to be a disturbing difference in perception here between the headteachers and the parents. One possible explanation is that parents feel inhibited from approaching schools for more information – they do not want to 'pester' hard-working teachers – but as a result are seen as apathetic and disinterested.

Finally, there is evidently a great deal of formal and informal contact between parents and schools, through such means as newsletters, parents' evenings and casual conversations with teachers. Yet it would appear that much of what is communicated through these contacts is of limited value for parents. The kind of information which parents seem to want – about what their children are doing and how they are getting on – does not seem to be communicated to them in a routine and effective manner. Instead, they must rely on what their children do and say to build up a picture of what is happening to them in school.

9

Parents and Assessment

At the end of the SATs, the teacher looked as if she could do with several large gins.

(Parent's comment)

The introduction of standardized assessment for all children aged 7, 11, 14 and 16 years has undoubtedly been one of the most controversial features of the current reforms. The idea has been vigorously promoted by politicians and policy-makers on the grounds that it is an essential part of raising standards; at the same time, it has been opposed with equal vigour by teachers and educationalists on the grounds that it is seriously flawed in practice. In this chapter we will briefly review the main arguments for and against standardized assessment, and then look at how it was actually experienced by the parents and children in our study.

The great assessment debate

Three main arguments have been put forward in support of standardized assessment. First, it is claimed that assessment will improve the quality of teaching and learning in the classroom by providing teachers with valuable information about children's progress. This argument was put forward in 1990 in a pamphlet for teachers entitled 'National Curriculum and Assessment' by the then Secretary of State for Education, John MacGregor:

A National Curriculum without assessment would have been lop-sided and incomplete. It would have lacked the dynamism – the potential to lever up standards – that assessment provides. . . . It is the means by which the teacher recognises the strengths and weaknesses of individual pupils, and is enabled to adapt his or her teaching to meet those needs so that strengths can be fostered and weaknesses tackled. (Department of Education and Science, 1990, p. 12)

The second main argument for assessment was also put forward by John MacGregor in the same pamphlet, when he claimed that the aggregated results of standardized assessments could be used to make public comparisons between the performance of individual schools or local authorities:

The information generated by the statutory assessments will, in aggregate, permit the performance of the education service as a whole, and that of individual schools, to be evaluated on a common basis. (p. 18)

As he was writing primarily for teachers, MacGregor did not put forward the third argument for assessment, that it can provide information for parents about their own child's progress. Nevertheless, this argument featured strongly in two government leaflets for parents entitled 'How is Your Child Doing at School?' (Department of Education and Science, 1991c, 1992). The 1991 version of this leaflet suggested that the main purpose of assessment was in fact to provide parents with detailed information about their own child's progress:

The point of the new tests is to give you and the teachers an exact picture of what your child has learned. Knowing how your child measures up against *national* standards will give you the best idea of his or her *real* progress. And knowing clearly your child's strengths and weaknesses will help you and the teacher to work together to meet his or her needs. When your child is tested again at age 11, you will see how far he or she has moved on. (p. 2 – emphasis in the original)

A number of arguments have been put forward against the introduction of standardized assessment. Many educationalists accept the first and third of the above arguments – that assessment may provide useful information for teachers and parents – but have queried the value of standardized assessment tasks (SATs) for this purpose. Paul Black, who was centrally involved in setting up the original ten-level structure for the National Curriculum and assessment, has argued that the use of short written tests is an inappropriate way to assess children's learning, and may well have undesirable side effects:

> The results will be unreliable, so they might harm individual pupils unless parents and schools decide to take little notice of them. Worse than this, the pressures on teachers to produce good results in such tests will lead them to drill pupils for them, which means learning by heart the atomised bits of knowledge that any such short tests are reduced to rewarding. (Black, 1992, p. 9)

Other educationalists have directed criticism at the second argument for assessment – namely, that the publication of assessment results can provide an objective basis for comparing the performance of schools. One argument is that the kind of measurement error which such tests inevitably contain renders them useless for this purpose:

> If we have the very reasonable assumption that Standardised Assessment Tasks (SATs) have an error of measurement of 3 per cent, then a betting man would discern no significant difference between the performance of Barnet at 16th and that of Tameside at 77th in the local education authority league table. In this sense, the table is meaningless. (Desforges, 1992)

It has also been argued that standardized assessment results are an inappropriate measure of a school's performance, as they take no account of the different abilities of pupils when they first enter school. In other words, a poor school with a high-ability intake might produce better 'objective' results than an excellent school with a low-ability intake. This argument has led certain newspapers to publish 'alternative league tables' which take account of this so-called 'value-added factor'.

Opposition from teachers has tended to focus more on the practicalities of the tests themselves. A survey of over 1,200 teachers who had taken part in the first standardized assessment of 7-year-olds found that the SATs had been unduly time-consuming, that normal teaching activities had been seriously disrupted, that children's behaviour had deteriorated, and that the SATs had told teachers little they did not already know (National Union of Teachers, 1991). A more extensive evaluation of the following year's assessments came to similar conclusions: teachers were concerned about the losses to teaching time caused by the SATs, about the disruption to their classrooms, about the dubious educational value of some of the tests, and about the increased stress and work-load generated by the SATs. The teachers in this survey were unanimously opposed to the SAT results being used for published league tables, and the overwhelming majority said that Teacher Assessment should be the principal form of assessment at Key Stage One (National Union of Teachers, 1992; see also Bennett et al. (1992) for further discussion of these issues).

Where do parents stand in this debate? It is often assumed by politicans and other supporters of the current reforms that parents are in favour of assessment. In April 1993 the Secretary of State for Education, John Patten, wrote in the *Daily Mail* that the testing of 7-year-olds and the publication of league tables had been 'welcomed by parents'. However, this welcome does not seem to have been universal. Some parents have organized local and national campaigns against standardized assessment, while other parents have actually withdrawn their children from school while the assessments were taking place – although this has not happened in England and Wales on the same scale that it has in Scotland. Moreover, the results of opinion polls published only the month after John Patten's statement suggested that there was growing opposition amongst parents to the formal assessment of their children (*The Independent*, 10 May 1993), and this opposition may well have influenced the modifications to government policy on assessment which were subsequently announced. As we saw in chapter 2, this uncertainty about whether parents support assessment was shared by the headteachers in our telephone survey: these heads tended to say either that their parents had mixed feelings on this issue or that they did not know what their parents thought.

The parents in our study provide a particularly valuable perspective on these issues. Their children were among the first cohort

of 7-year-olds to undergo standardized assessment in the summer
of 1991, and so both parents and children experienced the introduction of this controversial innovation at first hand. As one parent
aptly put it:

> We're all guinea pigs this time round – teachers, parents and
> children.

In the rest of this chapter we look at standardized assessment
from the viewpoint of the parents and their children. We focus on
four main issues:

- What did the parents know about the assessment process
  which the children were undergoing? Where did their
  knowledge come from? How much did the children know
  about what was happening?
- What did the parents feel about the SATs at the time? What
  effect did the SATs appear to have on their children?
- What did parents learn from the assessment process? What
  information were they given about their children? Did it tell
  them anything new?
- What was the parents' attitude towards assessment? Were
  their opinions changed by their experience of assessment?

In order to answer these questions, we will draw on the telephone interviews carried out with parents immediately after the
SATs were completed (see chapter 3), as well as on our annual
face-to-face interviews.

Parents' and children's awareness of the SATs

The 1991 assessment of 7-year-olds took place under a fierce glare
of media attention. Much of this attention focused on criticisms
of the SATs. Thus the media reported that the National Union of
Teachers (NUT) had passed a motion of opposition to the SATs
at its Easter conference and subsequently balloted its members
on a possible boycott, although in the end the boycott did not

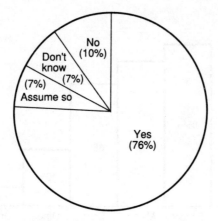

Figure 9.1 Were parents aware their child had been assessed?
(Telephone interviews, Year 3, *n* = 111.)

happen. The media also reported that the SATs were disrupting classrooms and causing children distress, while parents who withdrew their children from the SATs received a good deal of national publicity. Indeed, the media attention was so great that it seemed impossible not to be aware that all the 7-year-olds in the country were being assessed at that time.

Yet despite the large amount of publicity given to the SATs, there were still some parents in our study who seemed to have little or no awareness of what was going on. While the great majority of parents knew that their children had been assessed, or assumed it had happened, there were still some parents who said they did not know or that their children had not been assessed (see figure 9.1). Some parents were aware that 7-year-olds were due to be assessed at some point during the summer, but did not think it had happened yet, while others were not sure if their children were involved, possibly because they had not yet reached their seventh birthday. There were also a few parents who appeared to have no idea that any assessment was taking place at all.

Those parents who knew or thought that the assessments had taken place were asked where they had obtained this information. As figure 9.2 shows, most parents mentioned more than one source. The great majority of parents said they had heard about

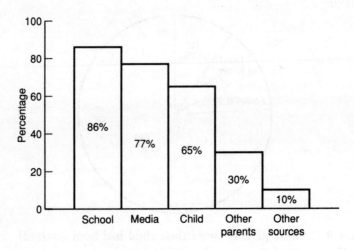

Figure 9.2   Parents' sources of information about the SATs (telephone interviews, Year 3, *n* = 92).

the assessments from the school, although it transpired that what they had been told varied considerably from school to school. Some parents appeared to have been given very full accounts of what was going to take place, usually through a parents' evening or newsletter, while other parents had been told little more than that the SATs were happening. Although this may simply have been an accident or oversight on the school's part, in some cases it was part of a deliberate policy to play down the SATs and provide minimal information about them. Indeed, some parents had been specifically asked not to mention anything about assessment to their children, on the grounds that the school was going to behave in a similar fashion.

Many parents obtained information about the SATs through their informal day-to-day contact with the school. In some cases parents were actually in the school helping out while the assessments were taking place. One parent had heard groups of children reading while other children were being assessed, while another parent, a classroom assistant at her child's school, had actually taken the class while the assessments were going on. In contrast, some parents had found out about the SATs almost by accident:

I went to pick him up for a dental appointment and he was half-way through one – the one with a box. Otherwise I wouldn't have known.

Just over three-quarters of the parents mentioned they had heard something about the SATs from the media (see figure 9.2). Their comments suggested that the media had focused primarily on the more controversial or problematic aspects of the SATs, and had not provided much in the way of detailed information about what was going on:

There was quite a lot on the telly – mostly about the teachers' resentment.

Just that parents are kicking up because it's upsetting the children.

Nearly two-thirds of the parents said they had heard something about the SATs from their children (see figure 9.2). Their comments gave some insight into how the children themselves were perceiving the SATs. In particular, there seemed to be considerable variation in the extent to which the children knew they were being assessed. Some children, it seemed, were very aware of what was going on, and even talked explicitly in terms of 'tests':

She said 'I had tests today. I had to choose from five books. I read part of the way through and was asked questions on it by the teacher. Then I went into another class and read some more.'

She said 'I did a test today Mummy – in water to see which things sink'. She was quite chuffed that she got them all.

Other children were apparently aware of something different happening at school, but did not seem to know they had actually been assessed. According to their parents, several children made reference to the fact that there had been a different teacher in their class during the assessment period, or that they had been doing 'special' activities, but none of these children explicitly mentioned being tested:

All she mentioned was that she was doing special group work. She didn't know they were tests. She just knew they were doing special things.

He said the teacher would be invisible for two days a week, and the children weren't to talk to her during that time unless they were with her – so he knew something different was happening.

A third group of children did not seem to have been aware of anything different happening at school. In some cases the parents had to infer from what their children said that the assessments had in fact taken place:

I heard nothing from her – I don't think she knew. I asked a couple of questions cautiously but she gave no indication that anything was going on.

Nothing except that he mentioned reading and answering questions. In a roundabout way I asked him but he appeared totally unaware – he hadn't noticed anything different.

Many parents had refrained from trying to extract information from their children for fear of putting pressure on them. Indeed, the parents' comments made a strong contrast with stories circulating at the time that anxious parents were deliberately 'coaching' their children for the SATs. There was little evidence that the parents in our study were doing anything of the sort – in fact they seemed more likely to be avoiding the issue in case they exerted undue pressure on their children. As one parent put it:

I didn't cross examine him too much, as I didn't want him to worry about it.

It would seem that there was considerable variation amongst the children in their awareness of the SATs. Some children were evidently very aware that they were being 'tested', while others appeared totally oblivious to the fact. While such variation amongst 7-year-olds is perhaps inevitable, it is also somewhat disturbing: it is widely recognized by developmental psychologists that a child's performance on a test is likely to be strongly influenced by their understanding of what the test is about, and in particular by their assumptions concerning the tester's purposes and intentions. The kind of variation in children's understandings suggested by our interviews raises serious questions as to whether the supposedly 'standardized' assessments were in fact anything of the sort.

There was also considerable variation in the parents' awareness of what was going on. At one extreme there were parents who were actually present in the classroom while the SATs were happening, while at the other extreme there were parents who did not even know their child had been assessed. Much of this variation, it would seem, was due to differences in the approach taken by the schools. Some schools opted for a policy of openly trying to keep everyone fully informed, while others tried to play down the SATs and treat them almost as if they were not happening. While there are clearly arguments for both approaches, it inevitably resulted in wide variation in parents' knowledge of what was going on.

Parents' and children's reactions to the SATs

The extensive media coverage of the 1991 SATs concentrated on two main issues. First, it was reported that many children had been upset by the assessment procedures, and that parents were consequently withdrawing their children from school when the SATs were taking place. Second, it was reported that many teachers considered the assessment procedures to be a waste of classroom time and that an NUT boycott of the tests was being considered. We therefore asked the parents how they felt about these two issues. We asked if their children had been upset by the SATs, and if they had contemplated withdrawing them from school during this period. We also asked if they thought the SATs had taken up too much teaching time, and whether they would have supported a boycott of SATs by the teachers.

Children's reactions to the SATs

Nearly two-thirds of the parents reported either that their children had a neutral reaction to the SATs or that they had no reaction

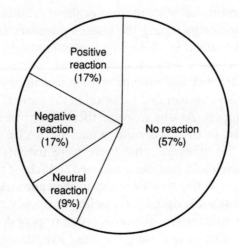

Figure 9.3 Children's reactions to the SATs (telephone interviews, Year 3, *n* = 92).

at all (see figure 9.3). Typically, they commented that their children had 'taken the SATs in their stride' or 'not been bothered by them'. However, about one in six of the parents reported that their children had reacted negatively to the SATs. These negative reactions were of two main kinds. Some children seemed to have been affected in a non-specific way, either by the SATs themselves or by the changes in classroom routine which the SATs had generated:

> She was very tired and anxious. I presumed it was pressure at school. She was tired, coming at the end of the half term, but maybe it was down to assessment.

> He said his teacher was not around a lot and that he was missing her.

Other parents reported that their children had been upset by specific incidents which had occurred during the assessments:

> She came home upset that she couldn't do some sums and her teacher wouldn't help her. She showed them once how to do them, but then wouldn't help any more. Her teacher usually helps them. It was the test – that was why.

She talked about one of the tests and realized that she'd made mistakes and was very concerned. I talked to her and said it wasn't the end of the world.

While the media accounts had led us to expect negative reactions such as these, we had not expected to find children who appeared to have responded positively to the SATs. In fact, positive reactions were reported just as frequently as negative reactions (see figure 9.3). These positive reactions took a variety of forms: some children enjoyed the extra attention, some enjoyed the challenge of being tested, while some even enjoyed the opportunity to beat the system.

I think she found it interesting. She enjoyed the teacher's attention in the little group.

I asked her and she said she had gone out of the classroom with others to do tests with the teacher. She liked it, liked the challenge.

He said it was his turn to choose a book to read and he'd gone to a different room to do it. It tickled him as he chose a book that he already knew.

Did parents consider withdrawing their children?

In order to gauge the strength of parents' feelings about the SATs, we asked them if they had considered withdrawing their children from school during this period. The great majority of parents (89%) said they had not seriously contemplated this. Many of these parents were unaware that it was possible, while others gave a variety of reasons:

I feel it's important for him to fit in – not be the odd one out.

He loves school. He'd hate staying at home.

If you put them to school, you go by the rules of school.

Some parents suggested that they might have responded differently if their child had been upset, or if another sibling was being assessed:

No. If it had affected her I would have done. If she had come home grumpy and obviously getting to her then I might have thought about it.

No. I was happy with my daughter, but I may not be so happy with my son. He's more of a worrier. Perhaps I would have thought more about it if it had been him.

Nearly 10 per cent of the parents said they had considered withdrawing their children from the SATs, although none of them had actually done so. Most of these parents seemed more concerned about the principle of assessment than about possible ill-effects to their child. It also seemed that in the end their objections were over-ruled by more practical concerns:

Yes. I discussed with other parents whether to withdraw them, but thought it would upset the staff too much, so I left it. See what happens this time around. Looks like a waste of time.

I thought vaguely about it as I am against the tests as such, but decided not to. Not to single him out was the reason.

I contemplated it especially prior to it. If they bring in written exams I would definitely withdraw my younger one. I thought it was bad enough at 11.

Did the SATs take up too much teaching time?

Another major issue which was raised by the media was that the SATs were taking up too much teaching time. It was reported that children's education was being seriously disrupted, as teachers devoted a large amount of time and energy to the SATs. We asked the parents if they felt this was true of their child's school. Although the question asked for the parents' own opinion on this issue, it was not always given: some parents told us instead what the teachers at the school felt about the SATs, and this was almost always negative:

When I spoke to the teacher she said it had taken a lot of time, even though she'd had a classroom assistant. She said she didn't really need to know what the SATs were revealing. They weren't telling her anything she didn't know already.

Among those parents who gave their own (rather than the teacher's) point of view, opinion was equally divided. Just over a third of these parents felt that the SATs had indeed been too time-consuming, typically saying that there had been periods during the SATs when their children did not seem to have received much teaching as the teachers' attention was elsewhere. Several parents also mentioned that the teachers appeared to have been been under severe pressure during this time, and some even suggested a possible remedy:

> Yes, it took a lot of preparation. The teachers looked exceedingly tired. It put an awful lot of pressure on them.

> At the end of the SATs, the teacher looked as if she could do with several large gins.

Other parents felt there had been substantial disruption to their children's education during this period, but were not sure how much this was directly due to the SATs:

> Disrupted but I'm not sure why. They've not had enough supervision. She's only had one reading book for 6 weeks so I feel she's lost out, but whether it's because of the SATs or because the teacher is the acting head I don't know.

Just under a third of the parents felt that the SATs had not taken up too much time. Typically, these parents commented that the children had still been learning anyway, or that the SATs enabled individual attention to be given to each child. There was also a sizeable group of parents who said they were unaware of any difference in the classroom during this period, or that they simply didn't know enough about was going on to venture an opinion.

While many parents displayed a good deal of sympathy towards the teachers, this did not necessarily extend to supporting a possible boycott of the SATs. Over three-quarters of the parents had heard about the NUT boycott, but less than a quarter said they approved of it. Those parents who said they would have supported it typically added that they had considerable trust in teachers' professional judgement, and that if the teachers had felt that a boycott was necessary, then they would have gone along with this decision:

> I was not surprised. If the teachers at this school had decided that I would have supported them. I would respect their decision as I have faith in them. I think teachers have had a raw deal.

Other parents were less supportive of teachers on this issue:

> I was disgusted. It (standardized assessment) is probably what all private schools have been doing for years. Teachers are so resistant to change.

The evidence presented here suggests that parents and children reacted to standardized assessment in a variety of ways. Some parents reported that their children had been upset by the SATs, while others said their children appeared to enjoy the experience. Some parents felt the SATs had disrupted classroom teaching, while others were not convinced this was so. Nevertheless, despite this variation, it is evident that the SATs had not been as straightforward or painless as many parents had been led to believe. Indeed, the unexpectedly disruptive nature of the assessment process had led many parents to question whether it was in fact worthwhile. This raises the question of what parents actually learned from the SATs, a question which we will shortly address. At the end of the chapter we look at whether parents felt the knowledge gained from the SATs had been worth the disruption caused.

How were the assessment results reported to parents?

After the children had been assessed, all the schools were formally required to supply parents with a written report containing their child's results. As we saw earlier, this part of the process is seen by the Government as being of central importance. The 1992 version of the leaflet for parents entitled 'How is Your Child Doing at School?' states that:

> As a parent you have a right to know how your child is doing at school. Under the Parent's Charter, all schools are now required to send you an annual report. That report must contain the results of National Curriculum tests, if your child has taken them. It must also contain other basic information about your child's progress. (Department of Education and Science, 1992, p. 7)

The leaflet also makes clear that the report should ideally be used by parents as the basis for discussion with teachers about how their child can best be helped:

> Just reading the report isn't the end of the story. As a parent you can use it to help you play an active part in your child's future education. The report will be a basis for talking to the teacher about your child's performance and his or her needs – and about how you can help. The school will be only too happy to talk to you about any of this. (p. 8)

In our final interviews with the parents we asked them how their child's assessment results had been reported to them. If they mentioned a written report, we asked them what it contained. We did not specifically ask to see the report, although many parents spontaneously brought it out and showed it to us. We also enquired whether the parents had been able to discuss the report with their child's teacher, and if so, whether they were happy with the discussion.

The great majority of parents (89 per cent) said they had received a written report containing their child's assessment results. However, there was a small group of parents (10 per cent) who said they had not been told their child's results. Further probing revealed that these parents had in fact received a written report which showed the assessment results in the standard form (i.e. as Levels 1, 2 or 3 in each of the three core subjects) but the parents had not realized that this was so. In some cases, the numbers had simply not registered with the parents, while in others the numbers had appeared meaningless and therefore been ignored. Our normal practice was to explain to these parents what the numbers meant, and then proceed with the interview.

There was considerable variation between schools in what was provided on the written report. The local education authority had produced a standard form which schools could use if they wanted, and several schools had done so: nevertheless, even those schools who had used the local education authority form had not necessarily completed it in the same way. Some schools gave the overall levels which children had reached in each subject, while others broke this down into specific profile components. Some schools augmented the levels with extensive comments about each child's progress in each subject, while others did not. One school gave no information about children's progress in music and religious education, even though there was space on the form for this; as a result, some parents assumed their children were not being taught these subjects when in fact they were. The local education authority form contained an optional sheet which allowed parents to make their comments on the report and agree a plan of action with their child's teacher: however, only one school in our sample made use of this facility. Other schools developed their own report form, or modified one they had used in previous years. The end result was that the nature and extent of the information which the parents were receiving about their child's progress varied considerably from school to school. As one parent said, after comparing her daughter's report with that of a friend at another school,

> You would have thought that if it's supposed to be a National Curriculum then all schools would have the same report.

As well as getting a written report, most parents (70 per cent) were also able to discuss the assessment results with their child's teacher. The majority of these parents said they were satisfied with the discussion, although there were familiar complaints about lack of time for discussion and poor timetabling (see chapter 8). There was also considerable variation from school to school in whether the opportunity for such discussion was made available and in how it was organized. Some schools deliberately sent out the report a few days before a parents' evening, so that parents had time to reflect on its contents, while other schools only handed out the report at the evening itself. One school made it clear that only those parents who were unhappy with the results should make an appointment to discuss them with the teacher, while other schools used the 'open-door' policy – if parents wanted to discuss the report they could always come in and do so. One school sent the report home two days before the end of term, thus effectively minimizing opportunities for discussion, although one parent considered this an improvement on previous practice:

> At least they gave us a day in which we could have contacted the teacher. They usually send it out on the very last day of term.

While all the parents had eventually received a written report containing their child's assessment results, there was evidently considerable variation from school to school in what the report contained, when it was sent out, and whether there was an adequate opportunity to discuss it with the teacher. While things may well have improved in subsequent years, at the time of our study there was clearly a major gap between the ideal scenario described in the Department of Education and Science leaflet and what was happening in practice.

What did parents learn from the reports?

We approached this question in various ways. We asked the parents whether they found the report easy to understand, and whether it had told them anything they did not already know. We also asked them if the results had been what they expected. For those parents who had been contacted by telephone immediately after the SATs, we were able to repeat back to them the predictions they had made at the time, and compare their predictions with the results their children had actually obtained. Finally, we asked the parents if they were happy with their children's results.

Most of the parents (77 per cent) said they found the written report easy to understand. A large amount of confusion, however, was caused by the numerical levels used to report the assessment results. Some parents were unclear whether Level 1 was higher than Level 3, while others had difficulty trying to match the levels with the written comments. A common complaint was that the levels were too broad to be meaningful, or that they were hard to interpret without knowing exactly what had been required of the children in the SATs. Those parents who had been given written comments found them more useful than the levels, although there were some complaints about the stereotyped nature of written comments: some parents felt that it was not very informative, for example, to be told their child's progress was 'satisfactory' in most subjects. At one school, a number of parents had compared the comments made on their children's reports and were irritated that the same phrases – such as 'needs to extend vocabulary' – were used repeatedly when describing different children.

Over two-thirds of the parents (70 per cent) felt they had not learnt anything new from the report. These parents typically commented that they already had a reasonably clear picture of their child's strengths and weaknesses, and that the report added little or nothing to that picture:

> No, I didn't learn anything new. If you keep in contact with the school during the term it's not that likely.

Just over a quarter of the parents (28 per cent) felt that the report had told them something new. Typically, they had learnt that their child had a particular strength or weakness which they had not previously been aware of. One parent, for example, told us that she hadn't realized how poor her daughter was at maths. She had worked with her on maths at home and felt she was doing fine. However, the assessments revealed that she was only at Level 1. Other parents commented that the results had enabled them to get a clearer picture of their child in relation to other children. One father described how his son had a learning problem, and because of this he felt he was more aware of his child's capabilities than he might otherwise have been. The father was working closely with the teacher on particular ways of helping his child. He felt that the SATs results just confirmed where his child stood in relation to his peers.

In general, the parents' answers to this question suggested that

Table 9.1   Children's 'actual' and 'expected' results (Year 3)

	English (n = 97)	Maths (n = 96)	Science (n = 92)
Did better than expected	22%	9%	24%
Did same as expected	65%	75%	68%
Did worse than expected	13%	16%	8%

their children's actual performance in the SATs had not been radically different from what they had expected. This suggestion was confirmed by a more detailed comparison of the children's 'expected' and 'actual' results. The 'expected' results were based on the predictions which parents made during the telephone interviews immediately after the SATs, while the 'actual' results were taken from what the parents told us in the final interviews.

As table 9.1 shows, the majority of children performed much as expected in each subject. There were some interesting variations from subject to subject, in that more children did better than expected in science and English than in maths, while fewer children did worse than expected in science. Overall, though, the results provide little evidence for the idea that parents tend to over-estimate their children's abilities. Instead, it seems that most parents have an accurate picture of their own child, and that where the picture is inaccurate it is at least as likely to be an under-estimate as an over-estimate.

The great majority of parents (81 per cent) said they were happy with their children's results. This is perhaps not surprising, given that most children did as well as, or even better than, their parents expected. One parent, for example, had expected her child to reach Level 2 in all subjects, and was quite content that he had done so. She commented:

> I was happy with his results. I'm not writing him off at 7 – it's just that, like I said to his teacher, I don't want a boy genius. He's a lad who enjoys himself. He's doing all right and that's as much as I want from him really.

Somewhat surprisingly, there were several parents who said they were happy with the results even though their child had not done as well as expected. A critical factor for most of these parents was whether they had been able to discuss their child's results with the teacher, and so obtain some sort of explanation for why their expectations had not been met. The following parent is typical of this group. She had expected her daughter to be at Level 2 in all subjects: however, while she reached this level in maths and science, she only reached Level 1 in English. After discussing the results with her daughter's teacher, she felt reassured:

> I was happy with the results. I discussed her English with her teacher, and she said that on her normal classwork she would be at Level 2, but that she didn't do too well on the test. I asked whether she needed extra help, and the teacher said I could always help at home, but that she's not below average.

While the great majority of parents were evidently happy with their children's results, there was a small but nonetheless important group of parents (18 per cent altogether) who either had mixed feelings or were unhappy with the results. Typically, their children had either done poorly on the assessments or had in some respect failed to match their expectations. One parent, for example, had expected her child to reach Level 2 in maths and science, although she was not sure she would be able to perform as well in English. In the end, her child was assessed at being at Level 1 in all three subjects:

> I wasn't happy with the report at all. I was surprised about the science, and I didn't realize she was so bad on the maths. I discussed it with the teacher. She was very helpful and told me what all her problems were, and about her concentration. She gave me a sheet as well on how to help her in the future. I agreed to help with her reading and maths.

Somewhat unexpectedly, there were a number of parents who said they were unhappy with the results even though their child had done as well as expected – or even better – in the SATs. In some cases their dissatisfaction was not so much with the results as such, but rather with the way the school had failed to communicate properly with them about their child's progress. One parent, for example, had expected her son to be at Level 2 in all subjects: in fact, he reached Level 2 in English and maths, and Level 3 in science. While this parent might have been expected to be pleased with his results, she was in fact upset by a comment the teacher had made on the report:

> I was put out by what the teacher said about his lack of concentration. When I asked before about him they said he was fine, but obviously he wasn't. It might just be a small thing but I felt misled. I could have worked on his concentration.

Another parent had commented during earlier interviews that she did not know enough about what her child was doing at school, or about how he was getting on. Her son was an only child and she remarked that she had nothing to compare him with, although she was surprised at how advanced some of his work seemed. He was one of the youngest in his class, and was only 6 when the assessments took place. Because of his youth, his mother was concerned that he would not do well in the SATs, and predicted that he would be at Level 1. In fact he reached Level 1 in English and maths, and Level 2 in science. Nevertheless, his mother said she was unhappy with the report:

> It's very detailed on him rather than his work. It's not constructive enough for us to do anything about. It's left us feeling that he's not doing very well and that he's not capable – that we've bred a little thickie.

The contents of this report had evidently provided a major shock to the parents concerned. Yet it must be emphasized that such cases were the exception rather than the rule. As we have seen throughout this section, parents were much more likely to say that the report had confirmed what they already knew than that they had learnt something of major import. Moreover, the great majority of parents seemed satisfied with what they had been told. For the minority who were not happy, the cause was only partly due to their child failing to meet their expectations; rather, their dissatisfaction seemed to stem as much from their feelings of not being kept adequately informed – and even of being actively misled – by their children's teachers.

Parents' attitude to assessment

In this section we look at the parents' attitude to assessment, and at the extent to which this was affected by their experience of SATs. We look first at whether parents approved of the general principle of assessing 7-year-olds, and at whether they thought written tests were appropriate for children of this age. We look at what parents felt about the publication of assessment results, and at whether they would move their child to a new school on the basis of such published results. Finally, we look at whether the parents would like an annual written report, and what they thought such a report should contain.

The parents' feelings about the principle of assessing 7-year-olds were generally more positive than negative. As figure 9.4

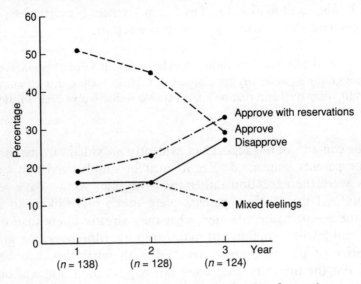

Figure 9.4   Parents' feelings about the principle of assessing 7-year-olds.

shows, around two-thirds of the parents each year either approved of assessment or approved with reservations. At the same time, there was an underlying trend of parents becoming more negative over the period of the study. The number of parents who approved unreservedly dropped substantially between Years 1 and 3, while there was a corresponding increase in those who approved with reservations and in those who disapproved. This negative shift was particularly pronounced between Years 2 and 3 – the period during which the SATs took place. In other words, while the parents were well disposed towards the idea of assessment before it happened, they became more critical as a direct result of their children being assessed.

Further insight into why this should be comes from the comments parents spontaneously made to justify their responses. In Year 1, those parents who supported assessment did so primarily on the grounds that it would provide information about children's strengths and weaknesses which could be used to guide future action. In particular, they wanted to know about areas in which they themselves could provide help at home:

To see what level the child's at. To see if they need extra help because they're below average or if they've excelled.

If there are problems we'll know before too late, and we can give more help.

There were relatively few mentions of other potential benefits for assessment, such as that it would 'keep teachers on their toes' or 'show up good or bad schools'. At the same time, a large number of concerns were expressed about the negative side of assessment, and particularly about the methods that might be used. Many parents were worried that the assessments would be done in too formal or rigid a way, particularly if these resulted in unnecessary pressure or stress on the children. A substantial number of parents felt that exam-like tests were inappropriate for children at this age: many recalled their own unhappy experiences of the 11-plus examination, and said they did not wish this on their own children. Concerns were also expressed about how the results would be used, about the dangers of labelling children, about the particular problems of children with special needs, and about the time and resources involved. Many of these concerns were put forward by parents who basically supported the principle of assessment:

> I approve hesitantly. It depends what the assessments are. Are we getting back to those awful tests at the end of term, when you could be labelled a failure just because your test performance was no good?

> Reluctantly. I'm not convinced the figures are going to be used in the right way.

> No, I'm not really in favour of it. Some children have got more brains than others. Children fall out at that age – it could be nasty if they start fighting and come home crying. They're too young to be assessed.

The responses given by parents at the end of the assessment process made it clear that, while some of their aspirations had been realized, so had many of their concerns. Parents expressed dismay at the time and resources which had been involved in SATs, and many had come round to the view that continuous assessment was a more appropriate method. There was also a substantial fall in the number of parents commenting that assessment would provide useful information to teachers and parents: this is hardly surprising, given that the majority of parents thought the assessments had not told them anything they did not already know. Above all, parents were increasingly coming to the opinion that 7 was 'too young' for the kind of assessment their children had experienced.

> I don't think it's really necessary at that age. Teachers know what each child is capable of. They know who needs help anyway.

> I still feel it's too young. They should be enjoying school at that age.

Some parents described specific experiences which had directly led to the change in their views. One father was strongly in

favour of assessment in Years 1 and 2. He favoured a more dis-
ciplined approach to education, and argued in Year 1 that exam-
like tests were good for children as they would 'make them think
at that time'. In Year 2 he was still strongly in favour of assessment,
commenting that:

> They need to be tested. This 'free' education isn't a good idea as
> they won't retain the education.

He expected his daughter to get Level 3 in all subjects in the
SATs, and felt that the school thought this was realistic. By the
Year 3 interview, however, his attitude had changed completely.
A key factor had been the day when his daughter came home
in tears after the maths SAT. She had not been able to do something and her teacher would not help her. The parents had found
this episode very upsetting, and it made them question the appro-
priateness of assessment at this age. The daughter eventually
received a Level 2 for maths, and the father felt this was not a true
reflection of her ability. By the Year 3 interview the father had
concluded that assessment was unfair at this age, as the children
were too young.

The parents' concerns about the methods used for assessing
7-year-olds also emerged when they were asked directly about
written tests. The parents were told during the Year 3 interview
that there were plans to place more emphasis in future years on
paper-and-pencil tests, and they were asked how they would have
felt about this for their own child. Just over half the parents (56
per cent) said they would not have been happy with this form of
assessment, compared with less than a third (28 per cent) who
would have been happy. Parents typically commented that this
would have put too much pressure on their child, that there was
too much variation in children's ability at this age, and that '7 is
too young'. Some of the parents who would have been happy for
written tests for their own child said that it would not have been
a good idea for other children:

> My own child could cope quite well, but others who are not so
> good at reading and writing would be put under pressure. It's not
> fair. There's enough pressure at the 11-plus.

The parents were also asked in Year 3 how they felt about assessment results being made public. As we have seen, the publication of assessment results in the form of 'league tables' is a crucial part of the current reforms. It is assumed that such tables will show which are good and bad schools, and hence put pressure on those schools who are not doing well to improve their performance. However, at the time of the final interviews such tables had not yet appeared, and it was difficult for many parents to grasp exactly what was meant. Some parents, for example, thought that the publication of assessment results for 7-year-olds would be similar to the publication of GCSE examination results in local newspapers, in that each child would be individually identified and their detailed results printed alongside their name.

Parents were divided on whether they approved of the publication of results. Just under half the parents (48 per cent) thought it was essentially a good idea – they felt that the publication of results would help to maintain standards, as well as influencing prospective parents:

> It's a good idea. If the results are bad, you can't change your choice, but you can put pressure on the school and find out why.

> They ought to publish results. It's one of the things we looked at when trying to find a school for the older one.

Some of these parents, however, felt that simply publishing the results on their own would be misleading unless other information was added:

> It would keep schools on their toes. But they should also give information about the background of the school and the children when presenting the results in public.

About one in five of the parents (19 per cent) were categorized as having 'mixed feelings', in the sense that they approved of publication in one form but not in another. As the following comments suggest, there was some variation in what parents felt was acceptable:

> It would be a good idea to publish the schools' results – it would
> fire up the teachers. But it's not fair on children if they're a bit
> slow but they've worked hard, and they then got stick from other
> children. That's not on.

> Not for individuals. Not for schools, even, that might put people's
> backs up a bit. But LEA areas would be OK. They can see where
> they're going wrong and put it right, instead of going on until 11
> and then thinking 'we're miles behind'.

Nearly a third of the parents (31 per cent) disapproved of the
idea of publishing assessment results. Some parents were particularly concerned about very small schools: they pointed out that
even if the school's results were aggregated it might still be possible
to identify individual children, or to blame a whole school's results
on the poor performance of one particular child. Other parents
were more straightforward in their objections to published results:

> It shouldn't be made that important. It could put too much pres-
> sure on children to get results. That wouldn't be good.

> I feel it should be between child, parent and teacher – it's no one
> else's business.

Some parents had clearly been influenced by their own child's
assessment results. Most of these parents were unhappy with the
results and did not feel they accurately portrayed their child's
abilities: in which case, they argued, how much value could you
place on the results of other children? Another parent, whose
child had reached Level 2 in English and maths and Level 3 in
science, had a slightly different reaction:

> I must admit I thought the assessment results would give me more
> information than they did. Schools are going to turn out so many
> average children, it will be difficult to see much between them in
> terms of quality of education.

The great majority of parents (81 per cent) said they would not
move their child to another school on the basis of published assessment results. Typically, these parents said that other things, such

as their child's happiness, were more important, or that such a move would be too disruptive for their child. Many parents pointed out that what mattered most was their own child's individual progress, not whether the overall results of the school were good or bad. One parent commented:

> I don't think I would. It's too much upheaval. And you could be forever moving them if the results change from year to year.

Of those parents who said they might move their child, three-quarters felt that published results would not be the only reason for such a move: their decision would depend on other factors as well. The few parents who said they would definitely move their child on the basis of published results made it clear that the results would have to be very bad for them to do this. Indeed, the parents' responses to this question provided little support for the idea that they would transfer in large numbers to schools which had obtained good assessment results.

The final issue we looked at was whether parents approved of the idea of an annual written report about their child's progress, as laid down in the Parent's Charter. It turned out that the parents were virtually unanimous that this was a good idea. A few parents qualified their response by saying they would rather have more personal contact with their child's teacher, or by pointing out that they had always had an annual written report from the school. Only one parent said they did not want a report:

> I don't think it's really necessary. It must have taken them such a long time to write something in each box. I think parents' evenings once a year are quite adequate.

The parents were also asked what sort of information they wanted the report to contain. The most popular request, made by over three-quarters of the parents, was for information about their child's progress in each subject. Over a third of the parents wanted information about their child's weaknesses, so they could provide help at home. There were also a significant number of requests for information about their child's behaviour, social skills and attitude to work. However, only one in ten of the parents wanted to know their child's position in the class relative to other children. There were also few requests for general information about the school, such as truancy rates.

Overview

This chapter has focused on the controversial issue of standardized assessment. We have looked at how far the parents and children in our study were aware of the assessment process, and at how they reacted to the SATs. We have also looked at what the parents learned from the reporting of assessment results, and the effect that the whole process had on their attitudes towards assessment. Two main issues emerge.

First, there would seem to be a major question over how far the standardized assessments could actually be considered to be 'standardized'. There appeared to be large variations in what the parents and children were told about what was going on, in how the SATs were organized and carried out, and in how the results where reported to parents. The idea that all children went through the same process, and that all parents ended up with the same type of information, was simply not borne out by our interviews. While such unevenness in procedures is perhaps inevitable at the start of a major innovation, our findings are still worrying given the importance that has been attached to the results and the ensuing 'league tables'.

Second, our findings raise serious doubts about whether the whole assessment and reporting process was actually providing what parents wanted. There is substantial evidence, both from this chapter and the previous one, that parents have a strong desire for accurate and up-to-date information about how their children are getting on at school. In particular, they want to know about their children's strengths and weaknesses so they can provide help where necessary at home. At the start of the study, many parents were in favour of assessment because they felt it would provide them with this sort of detailed and usable information about their children. By the end of the assessment and reporting process, however, over two-thirds of the parents were saying they had not learnt anything new as a result of the SATs. It is hardly surprising that parents were significantly more negative about assessment at the end of the study than they had been at the beginning: the SATs had simply failed to deliver.

10
Giving Parents a Voice

If they ask for our opinion they must use it.
(Parent's comment on being consulted by the school)

The current reforms have placed parents at the centre of the educational stage. The success or failure of the reforms depends crucially on how far parents will play their new role as consumers of education. And yet, as we saw in chapter 1, this role has been handed to parents with a minimal amount of consultation about how they want to play it, or even whether they want to play it at all. It is a curious irony that while parents have been given unprecedented power and influence by the reforms, they have not been given an effective voice.

In this book we have enabled a particular group of parents to voice their views on a wide range of issues. These parents were chosen because they are in many ways the pioneers of the current reforms: their children were among the first to receive the National Curriculum at Key Stage One, and they took part in the first standardized assessment of 7-year-olds ever carried out in this country. What these parents have to say about the National Curriculum and assessment, about their new role as consumers, and about other aspects of the reforms is therefore of prime importance for anyone involved in education today. In this final chapter we will summarize what the parents are saying, and put forward some implications for policy and practice.

The findings

Our research has focused on six main areas in which assumptions about parents underlie the current reforms. In each area we have shown that the assumptions being made do not necessarily agree with what the parents in our study are saying. Indeed, it appears that on some issues there is a serious gap between what is assumed about parents and how they actually think and behave.

Issue 1: Parents as consumers   One of the central assumptions underlying the current reforms is that parents should be seen as consumers of education. We saw in chapter 4, however, that there was considerable reluctance amongst the parents towards taking on this new role. Only a small minority of parents saw themselves 'very much' as consumers, and many parents found the idea puzzling or difficult to apply to their particular circumstances. While there was a steady rise during the period of the study in the number of parents who saw themselves 'to some extent' as consumers, there were still many parents who qualified this by saying that education could not be reduced to simple market terms. Furthermore, while parents primarily saw the role of consumer as being concerned with the initial choice of school, it was also seen by many in terms of their continuing relationship with the school once the initial choice had been made.

Issue 2: Parental choice   The consumerist model assumes that parents will make considered choices between schools on the basis of published information about academic standards. We saw in chapter 5, however, that this model was of only limited applicability to the parents in our study. For example, there were some parents who did not have any realistic choice of school, either because they could not travel to other schools or because the other schools were full. There were also a substantial number of parents who did have the possibility of choice but who did not make use of it: typically, these parents were happy with what the local school provided and saw no reason to look elsewhere. And although there were undoubtedly many parents who considered more than one school, some of these parents were forced into looking elsewhere, either because they could not get into the school of their choice or because they had heard unfavourable reports about the local school. All in all, there were relatively few parents whose behaviour when choosing schools appeared to fit the pure consumerist model.

Our research also cast doubt on the assumption that parents will choose schools purely on the basis of academic performance. The findings reported in chapter 5 suggest that other factors – such as a school's location, size or friendliness – are of equal, if not greater, importance. A similar picture emerged in chapter 6, when parents were asked directly what they considered to make a good school: factors such as relationships, atmosphere and ethos featured much more prominently than academic results. We also saw in chapter 9 that the great majority of parents would not move their children purely on the basis of published assessment results. Overall, our research provides little support for the assumption that parents are solely concerned with academic results.

Issue 3: Parental satisfaction   Another assumption underlying the current reforms is that parents are deeply dissatisfied with their children's schools, and particularly with the standards which prevail. Our research provides little evidence to support this assumption (see chapter 6). Each year the vast majority of parents said they were happy with their child's school and that the teachers were doing a good job. Over three-quarters of the parents were happy with their children's progress in English and maths, and only a handful of parents moved their children because they were unhappy with the school. These figures do not suggest widespread dissatisfaction amongst parents: rather, they indicate general approval of schools as they are at present, and a significant appreciation of the job which teachers are doing.

We also found that parents were much more likely to express concern about 'standards' in general than about those at their own child's school. This finding suggests that, where parents have to rely on second-hand information about schools in general, they are more likely to reflect the concerns about standards which are regularly expressed in the media. On the other hand, where they can draw on their personal experience of their child's particular school, then they are much more likely to respond in positive terms.

Issue 4: Parents and the National Curriculum   It is widely assumed that parents approve of the National Curriculum, and of the emphasis placed on English, maths and science at its core. Yet the evidence presented in chapter 7 provides only limited support for these assumptions. While the majority of parents were in favour of the National Curriculum, many expressed concerns about it, both in principle and in practice. And while the majority of parents were in favour of having English, maths and science at the core, many felt this focus on the basics was too limiting. We also found little support for the idea that parents want a wholesale return to traditional teaching methods: parents were just as likely to advocate practical approaches, or to emphasize that learning at this age should be interesting and fun.

Issue 5: Parents' knowledge about school   One argument frequently put forward in support of the National Curriculum and standardized assessment is that they will increase parents' knowledge of what goes on at school – a view which was shared by the parents at the beginning of the study. However, the findings reported in chapter 8 suggest that the reforms have so far made little impact on the level of parents' knowledge. Most parents felt they knew little about what their children were learning in school, and their knowledge about the National Curriculum and assessment was also limited. This did not seem to be due to lack of interest, as the parents repeatedly said they wanted to know more about such matters. Nor was it due to lack of contact with the school, as this also seemed plentiful. Rather, it appeared that the contacts parents had with the school were not providing them with the information they needed, and many were relying on their child as their main source of information.

Issue 6: Parents and assessment   It has often been assumed that parents support standardized assessment, on the grounds that it will raise standards and provide useful information about the performance of their children and the school. In fact, the parents in our study became increasingly negative towards assessment as the study wore on (see chapter 9). At the start of the study most of the parents approved of assessment, primarily on the grounds that the information provided would enable them to help their children at home. Their actual experience of SATs, however, led many of them to revise their views. The SATs themselves were frequently seen as disruptive and time-consuming, and over two-thirds of the parents felt they had not learned anything new as a result of the process – a view supported by the close correlation between their children's 'expected' and 'actual' results. Moreover, the parents' accounts of assessment and reporting revealed just how much variation there was in a supposedly standardized procedure.

In summary, our research suggests that many of the assumptions about parents which underlie the current reforms do not match closely with the real views, experiences and behaviour of the parents most directly involved. In particular, the idea that parents should be seen as consumers – in the narrow, market sense of the term – does not seem the most appropriate description of the parents in our study. Nor could we find much evidence that these parents should be regarded as 'problems', in the sense that they lacked interest in their children's education: on the contrary, we were repeatedly struck by the intense concern with which parents from all social backgrounds talked about their children and their education. Rather, we were left with the strong impression of a group of parents whose interest and concern for their children's education was not always being recognized by the designers and providers of that education.

How far will the findings generalize?

Before we turn to the implications of our findings for policy and practice, a number of qualifications need to be made about the present study.

1 The size of the sample is by some standards relatively small. As we pointed out in chapter 3, we deliberately sacrificed quantity for quality, aiming for an in-depth study of a manageable number of parents rather than a more superficial study of a larger number.

2   The parents were all drawn from one part of the country, and it is possible that parents elsewhere in the country may have different views. In particular, the sample contained relatively few parents from ethnic minorities. It did, however, contain parents from a wide range of socio-economic circumstances, including some living in deprived inner-city areas.

3   The parents were interviewed at a relatively early stage of their children's education (5–7 years). It is possible that their views and priorities might change as their children got older, and that they might become more concerned with academic standards and less concerned with other factors.

4   One of the strengths of the study – that it is based around parents who were pioneers of the National Curriculum – might also be seen as a weakness. It could be argued that these parents are experiencing the reforms at their 'teething' stage, and that subsequent generations of parents may respond more favourably when the reforms have been up and running for a few years.

5   The parents were all drawn from the state sector (although a few moved their children to private school during the course of the study). It is possible that parents using the private sector might have very different views on some of these issues, such as consumerism and what they consider to make a good school.

These qualifications should be taken seriously. They raise important questions about how far the findings of the present study can be generalized to other groups of parents, in other locations, at other points in time. Nevertheless, these are questions for further research rather than major criticisms of the study. Despite the huge amount of time and resources which has been invested in the current reforms, and despite the central importance of parents to these reforms, there has been remarkably little publicly funded research on how parents are responding to what is going on. Until that research is funded and carried out, we must rely on the present study, with all its qualifications, as a prime source of evidence about parents' views.

Furthermore, as we have noted at various points in the book, many of our findings fit closely with those of other research, carried out both before and after the current reforms were introduced. For example, our finding of widespread parental satisfaction is supported by studies of infant schools (Tizard et al., 1988), junior schools (Mortimore et al., 1988) and secondary schools (West, Davies and Scott, 1992), as well as by the Department of Education and Science funded survey of parents at all levels of education (Public Attitude Surveys, 1989). Many of our findings have also been confirmed and extended by a further study of parents and assessment at Key Stage One, in which one of us is currently involved (Holden, Hughes and Desforges, 1993); this study involves parents from ethnic minorities in London and Bristol as well as parents from the southwest. Moreover, there are strong resonances between some of our findings and research carried out in Canada (Coleman, Collinge and Tabin, 1993), Australia (Toomey, 1993) and New Zealand (Ramsay et al., 1990) despite major differences between the education systems in these countries. In other words, while our findings need to be replicated and extended, they do not seem very discrepant with what has been reported elsewhere.

Parents differ

One further qualification to our findings which should be stressed is that of individual differences: parents do not speak with a single voice. At various places in the book we have seen considerable variation amongst parents on particular issues, such as the extent to which they saw themselves as consumers, in the amount of choice they exercised, and in their attitudes to the National Curriculum and assessment. Even on issues where the great majority of parents agreed – such as their satisfaction with the school or their appreciation of teachers – there were still a few parents who did not fit the overall picture. Moreover, parents do not necessarily say the same thing from one year to the next: most notably, there were significant changes during the period of the study in parents' perceptions of themselves as consumers and in their attitude to assessment. Diversity and change, it would seem, are important features of parents' views.

We have not attempted here to examine systematically what underlies this diversity in parents' views: that would be a major undertaking in itself, requiring time and resources well beyond those currently available to us. Nevertheless, the impression gained from our interviews is that at least three types of factor seem to be involved.

First, there are factors which are deeply rooted in the parents themselves: these include the more obvious characteristics such as gender, ethnicity and social class, as well as the parents' own experiences of education, their aspirations for their children, their beliefs about the wider purposes of education, and their political views about the kind of society they want to live in. The second set of factors consists of the particular circumstances in which parents currently find themselves: these include external factors such as the range and quality of schools currently available in their locality, or whether there is suitable public transport to extend their choice, as well as more personal factors such as their current employment (or lack of it), the state of their health or marriage, and whether they can afford private education. The final set of factors consists of the specific experiences which parents have with particular schools, such as whether their children seem to be making adequate progress, how they or their child relate to a particular teacher, or the extent to which they feel welcome in the school. Our interviews suggest that it is the complex interplay of these different sorts of factors which underlies and shapes the particular views expressed by individual parents.

Implications for schools

The overriding message from our research as far as headteachers and teachers are concerned is a positive one – parents are much more appreciative and satisfied than one might imagine! In contrast to the picture frequently painted by politicians and the media, we found little evidence that parents were dissatisfied with their children's schools or the standards which prevailed. Instead, the picture which emerged was one of widespread satisfaction, combined with a significant appreciation of the job which teachers are doing.

This will undoubtedly be a welcome message for teachers. After several years of externally imposed change, high levels of stress and constant criticism in the media, it is hardly surprising that many teachers have come to doubt whether they still have the support of their parents. Our research suggests that they do: while parents may not be aware of the finer points of the National Curriculum or assessment procedures, they are well aware of the effects which these changes have had on teachers and of the difficulties in which they are currently operating. The parent who commented that her child's teachers were 'brilliant under difficult circumstances' doubtless spoke for many.

At the same time, our research does not provide practitioners with any grounds for complacency. Many parents expressed criticisms or reservations about their children's schools at some point or other during the study. Individual concerns were voiced about progress, discipline, communication between home and school, the lack of response to complaints, the poor physical condition of the school, overcrowding and headlice. In addition, there was a widespread feeling that not enough was being done to keep them informed. These are important concerns which should not be ignored.

Indeed, it is clear that in the current climate schools which choose to ignore the concerns of their parents do so at their peril. The new funding arrangements for schools, the move towards greater accountability at local level, and the new rights given to parents under the Parent's Charter leave little doubt that schools must increasingly be prepared to listen to the views of their parents and, where possible, to take on board what they are saying. This does not mean that schools should simply provide whatever parents happen to want, out of fear that if they do not, then the parents will move their child to another school: our research suggests that relatively few parents behave like that in practice. What it does mean is that schools should continue their efforts to build genuine partnerships with their parents, based on mutual respect and a clear understanding of the other partner's point of view.

What might this mean in practice? Such a question is not easy
to answer: what works in one school may be totally inappropriate
in another. Nevertheless, a good starting place would be for schools
to carry out a fundamental review of all aspects of their current
relationship with parents. This review might be limited to a few
members of staff with particular responsibility for working with
parents, or it could involve wide-ranging discussions involving
all teaching and non-teaching staff, governors and even some parents. While it is clearly up to each school to set its own agenda,
our research suggests that the following questions might usefully
be addressed:

- **Perceptions**   How does the school perceive its parents?
  How are they talked about in the staffroom? Are they seen
  as consumers, as problems or as partners? What evidence are
  these perceptions based on?
- **Messages**   What messages does the school actually give
  out to parents? How far are they made to feel valued and
  important members of the school? Does the way parents are
  treated on a day-to-day basis fit with the school's overall
  policy towards parents? Are they excluded from certain areas
  of the school, and if so why?
- **Voice**   What opportunities do parents have to give voice
  to their views? How many parents actually take up these
  opportunities? What happens when they do? How far is the
  school influenced by a few parents who are highly vocal, at
  the expense of the 'silent majority'?
- **Choice**   Why do parents choose the school? What alternatives do they have? What is the school's reputation in the
  community? How accurate is it? If the school wanted to
  change its reputation, how could it go about doing so?
- **Values**   What do parents think 'makes a good school'?
  What sort of education do they want for their children?
  What is the degree of overlap between the parents' values
  and those of the school?
- **Satisfaction**   How happy are parents with the school?
  What do they like about it? What do they dislike? What
  methods are there for parents to express their appreciation?
  What methods are there for parents to express their concerns?

- **Information**   How much do parents know about what is happening to their children in school? How do they find out? What methods are currently used to inform parents? Are these methods successful? If not, why not?
- **Progress**   How are parents kept informed about their child's progress? Do they have an adequate and accurate picture of how their child is progressing? What methods exist for parents to express concern about their child's progress? How does the school respond when they do?
- **Involvement**   What does the school mean by 'involving parents'? In what ways are parents currently involved? Are all parents involved, or is it just a minority? Do parents want to be more involved, or are they happy with the current situation?

Doubtless, there will be many schools who feel they already know the answers to these and similar questions. But equally, there will be many who come to realize in the course of such a review that their knowledge of the parents' perspective is far from complete. Such schools might then want to engage in some sort of systematic enquiry into their parents' views, similar to the one described in this book. If so, they might find the following useful.

Obtaining parents' views

There are two main ways by which schools can find out their parents' views – the questionnaire and the face-to-face interview. Questionnaires, which ask parents to complete and return a sheet of written questions, are undoubtedly the quickest and easiest way to get a large amount of information. One disadvantage of questionnaires, though, is that they are relatively impersonal and inflexible, although this can be countered by leaving space for parents to write in personal comments. Another disadvantage is that they may not be returned by those parents from whom the school may particularly want to hear, such as those for whom English is not their first language. Interviews, in contrast, allow for more in-depth and personal probing of issues, but are much more time-consuming. The best method may well be a combination of the two, in which a general questionnaire is sent out to all parents, followed by in-depth interviews which focus on particular issues and target particular groups of parents (or a cross-section of them).

Whatever method is employed, time and care needs to be spent on designing the specific questions to be asked. These should reflect a genuine desire on the part of the school for the information which is being asked for – there is little point in a school surveying its parents if it is only interested in being told how well it is doing. The questionnaire or interview schedule must also be looked at closely from the parent's point of view – the questions should be clear and unambiguous, and ideally allow for several different types of response. A useful contrast might be drawn here with the standard questionnaire for parents which is part of the current Office for Standards in Education (OFSTED) inspection arrangements, and which allows only for yes/no answers.

Responding to parents' views

Having obtained the views of their parents, schools must then make crucial decisions about whether and how far they want to implement what parents want, particularly when it does not agree with the school's current ethos or ideology. This is clearly a decision which each school has to make for itself, and one which it is tempting to leave until the data-gathering from parents is over. However, there is a great danger of raising parents' expectations by engaging in a consultation process but then failing to act on the results of the consultation. As one parent in our study put it: 'If they ask for our opinion they must use it'.

There are many examples of schools which have consulted their parents on a specific issue or set of issues and then put the results of their consultation into practice. This is particularly so in Scotland, where it has been widely encouraged as part of a major project on school self-evaluation carried out by the Scottish Office Education Department (McGlynn and MacBeath, 1992). But there are also examples, both published and unpublished, from other parts of the UK. For example:

One of the schools in our study had a poor reputation with its parents shortly before the study began. The school embarked on a major consultation process, in which it emerged that parents had concerns about the 11-plus which still existed in the area. As a result, the school introduced voluntary homework for its older pupils, even though the head did not personally approve. Several parents said they were much more impressed by the fact that the school had listened to them than by the actual introduction of homework.

A junior school in Birmingham decided on the format of the school report by asking parents exactly what they wanted to know about their children. According to the headteacher, the school was surprised to find that the parents wanted to know as much about their child's personal and social development as they did about their academic progress (Morton, 1991).

The governors of a large community school in the southwest interviewed a sample of their parents on a wide range of issues, such as their perceptions of the school and their attitudes towards discipline. The governors realized through this how much they had erroneously assumed about their parents, and particularly about the parents' knowledge of school procedures. As a result, the governors embarked on a process of informing parents about the school.

The majority of parents at a small primary school in Devon signed a petition opposing league tables of SAT results. The petition was discussed at length at a governors' meeting at the school. The governors decided their first loyalty was to the parents and the children, and so agreed not to send in the SAT results (Holden, 1993).

What is common to each of these examples is that the schools concerned did not regard their parents as a potential threat who should be kept at arm's length, but as an important group of people whose views were of direct relevance to the life of the school. We hope that many more schools will feel encouraged by such examples, and by the findings of our research, to approach their parents in a similar way.

Of course, schools do not have to carry out full-scale consultations with their parents to demonstrate that they value parents and are prepared to treat them with respect. Such an attitude can be conveyed though a variety of small actions, ranging from the wording of a notice or letter for parents to the way the school deals with complaints. This last point is well illustrated by two parents in our study, who both complained to the headteacher that their child was being bullied. In one school, the head simply said he would deal with it but the parent heard nothing more about the matter. In the other school, the head not only dealt with the bullying but reported back to the parent about how she had done so: this head also explained some of the personal problems facing the child who was bullying, thus making the parent more aware of the circumstances underlying the problem. It is perhaps no coincidence that the first parent subsequently moved her child from the school, while the second did not.

Implications for policy

We return to the issue with which this book has been centrally concerned – the role which parents have been given by politicians and policy-makers in the current educational reforms. As we have seen throughout the book, our research has revealed a number of serious discrepancies between the assumptions about parents which underlie the reforms and the views of the parents who are most directly involved. In particular, our research raises considerable doubts as to whether politicians and policy-makers can continue to justify the reforms on the grounds that they 'provide what parents want'. Our findings suggest that in many crucial areas – such as consumerism, choice, satisfaction and assessment – these justifications can no longer be sustained.

Politicians and policy-makers are thus faced with two main alternatives. On the one hand, they can continue the reforms in their current direction, regardless of whether or not they have the support of parents. The reforms would then have to be justified by some other argument – for example, that they were raising educational standards, or that they were supported by teachers. Alternatively, those responsible for educational policy can accept that parents have a legitimate voice in the development of that policy, and embark on a series of consultations with parents' organizations – and with individual parents – in order to hear their views on the reforms so far and on how they should be developed further. At the time of writing (summer 1993) there are some signs that this listening process is under way, as part of the review of the National Curriculum being undertaken by Sir Ron Dearing, and it seems likely that some of the most recent modifications to the assessment procedures represent at least a partial recognition of parents' concerns on this issue. However, whether parents will play a longer-term and more substantial role in the development of policy remains to be seen.

What might the agenda be for such consultations between parents and policy-makers? What issues should they be addressing? While both sides in the discussions would doubtless have their own particular concerns, we believe that the six main issues which have featured in this book should form a prominent part of the agenda. In particular, we believe that the following issues and questions should be directly addressed:

- **Consumerism: How far should parents be considered as consumers of education?** Our research suggests that many parents – and headteachers – are uncomfortable with the narrow market model of consumerism which has dominated the reforms to date. Is it not time to move away from this model and develop a broader conception of what it means to be a consumer – perhaps based on Woods' (1993) notion of the consumer-citizen – which emphasizes parents' ongoing relationship with the school once they have made their initial choice? If so, what rights would parents have under this model? And what would be their responsibilities?
- **Choice: How important is parental choice?** Our research suggests that the consumerist model of how parents choose schools does not fit closely with the realities of parents' lives. Is it not time, then, to reconsider the prime

place which choice has been given within educational policy? How can a policy based on choice deal with those parents who in reality have no choice? Do parents and policy-makers really want the two-tier system which seems to be emerging, in which a few schools choose their parents while the rest desperately fight for survival? How much choice do parents actually want – or need?

- **Satisfaction: What do parents want from schools – and are they getting it?**   Our findings suggest that parents are less concerned with academic standards than with other aspects of education. If so, then how can educational policy be developed so that it more accurately reflects parents' wishes? Our research also casts doubt on the widely held assumption that parents are dissatisfied with schools and the standards that prevail. In that case, how has this false assumption arisen? What role has the media played in promoting the idea of parental dissatisfaction – and how can parents ensure that their views are accurately portrayed by the media?

- **National Curriculum: What should be taught in schools, and who should decide?**   Our research suggests there is only moderate enthusiasm for the National Curriculum amongst parents, as well as a feeling that its focus on the basics might be too limiting. But how can parents' views on what should be taught be incorporated in a curriculum which is decided at national level? Should we rather be aiming for more diversity from school to school, allowing parents to have more say in the curricula of individual schools? And what about teaching methods – should parents have a say on this issue too, or should it be left purely to the professionals?

- **Knowledge: Do parents know enough about what is happening in their children's schools?**   Our research suggests they do not. Moroever, we found that the kind of information which parents want is much more immediate and personalized than that provided by National Curriculum documents or the results of standardized assessments. Parents want to know what and how their child is doing this week – so they can talk about it at home and provide help where needed. How can schools best provide this sort of information? And whose responsibility should it be to keep parents informed about current developments in education?

- **Assessment: How should parents be kept informed about their children's progress?** Is it necessary – or even appropriate – for children to receive regular standardized assessment? How far can parents rely on teachers' own assessments? Our research suggests that parents support assessment if they think it will provide useful information about their child's strengths and weaknesses – and SATs do not necessarily do this. How can an assessment system be devised which tells parents what they really want to know?

We do not pretend that discussions between policy-makers and parents on these issues are likely to result in clear agreement – indeed, our research suggests that policy-makers and parents will provide very different answers to these and similar questions. Our point is rather that if policy-makers genuinely want to maintain that their policies are supported by parents, then they must give parents a central role in the decision-making process, and listen to what parents are really saying on these issues.

We conclude by restating the main theme of the book. Assumptions are constantly made about parents by all those who are involved in education. These assumptions range from statements by politicians that 'parents want higher standards' or 'parents support assessment' to the comments of individual headteachers that 'parents are disinterested' or 'apathetic'. Our research suggests that many of these assumptions do not coincide with what real parents actually do, say or think. We believe it is crucial that all those involved in education – whether they be Secretaries of State, policy-makers, headteachers or teachers – should reflect carefully on their assumptions about parents, and consider how far these assumptions are supported by the available evidence. It is right that parents should have a voice in their children's education – it is also right that the designers and providers of that education should listen carefully to what parents are saying.

References

Alexander, R., Rose, J. and Woodhead, C. 1992: *Curriculum Organisation and Classroom Practice in Primary Schools*. London: DES.

Bash, L. and Coulby, D. 1989: *The Education Reform Act: Competition and Control*. London: Cassell.

Becher, T., Eraut, M. and Knight, J. 1981: *Policies for Educational Accountability*. London: Heinemann.

Bennett, S.N., Wragg, E.C., Carré, C.G. and Carter, D.S.G. 1992: A longitudinal study of primary teachers' perceived competence in, and concerns about, National Curriculum implementation. *Research Papers in Education*, 7, 53–78.

Bernstein, B. 1971: *Class, Codes and Control*. London: Routledge.

Black, P. 1992: Introduction to *Education: Putting the Record Straight*. Stafford: Network Educational Press, 5–12.

Board of Education 1931: *Report of the Consultative Committee on the Primary School* (Hadow Report). London: HMSO.

Brown, P. 1991: The 'third wave': education and the ideology of parentocracy. *British Journal of Sociology of Education*, 11, 65–85.

Central Advisory Committee for Education 1967: *Children and their Primary Schools* (Plowden Report). London: HMSO.

Coleman, P., Collinge, J. and Tabin, Y. 1993: The learning triad: rethinking the co-production of learning project on family and school collaboration in instruction in British Columbia. In R. Merttens, D. Mayers, A. Brown and J. Vass (eds) *Ruling the Margins: Problematising Parental Involvement*, London: University of North London Press, 97–119.

Corrigan, P. 1988: GERBIL: The Education Reform Bill. *Capital and Class*, 35 (Summer).

Cox, C.B. and Boyson, R. (eds) 1977: *Black Paper 1977*. London: Temple Smith.

Cyster, R., Clift, P.S. and Battle, S. 1979: *Parental Involvement in Primary Schools*. Windsor: National Foundation for Educational Research.

David, M.E. 1993: *Parents, Gender and Education Reform*. Cambridge: Polity Press.

Department for Education 1992: *Choice and Diversity: A New Framework for Schools* (Education White Paper). London: HMSO.

Department of Education and Science 1975: *A Language for Life* (Bullock Report). London: HMSO.

Department of Education and Science 1988: *Our Changing Schools: A Handbook for Parents*. London: DES.

Department of Education and Science 1990: *National Curriculum and Assessment*. London: DES.

Department of Education and Science 1991a: *The Parent's Charter*. London: DES.

Department of Education and Science 1991b: *Your Child and the National Curriculum*. London: DES.

Department of Education and Science 1991c, 1992: *How is Your Child Doing at School?* London: DES.

Desforges, C. 1992: Trends in primary education. Paper presented at the North of England Conference, Southport.

Docking, J.W. 1990: *Primary Schools and Parents*. London: Hodder and Stoughton.

Douglas, J.W.B. 1964: *The Home and the School*. London: Macgibbon and Kee.

Edwards, A. and Whitty, G. 1992: Parental choice and educational reform in Britain and the United States. *British Journal of Educational Studies*, 30, 101–17.

Flew, A. 1987: *Power to the Parents*. London: Sherwood Press.

Golby, M. and Lane, B. 1989: *The New School Governors*. Tiverton: Fairway Publications.

Gooch, M. 1990: Home truths on the role of parents. *The Guardian*, 24 July.

Graham, D. 1992: The elusiveness of quality. In *Education: Putting the Record Straight*, Stafford: Network Educational Press, 33–7.

Griffiths, A. and Hamilton, D. 1984: *Parent, Teacher, Child*. London: Methuen.

Hannon, P. and Jackson, A. 1987: *The Belfield Reading Project*. London: National Children's Bureau.

Hillgate Group 1986: *Whose Schools? A Radical Manifesto*. London: Claridge Press.

Hillgate Group 1987: *Reform of British Education*. London: Claridge Press.

Holden, C. 1993: Dilemma in deepest Devon. *Education*, 4 June.

Holden, C., Hughes, M. and Desforges, C.W. 1993: What do parents want from assessment? *Education 3–13*, 21, 3–7.

Hughes, M. 1986: *Children and Number.* Oxford: Basil Blackwell.

Hughes, M. 1994: The oral language of young children. In D. Wray and J. Medwell (eds) *Teaching Primary English: The State of the Art*, London: Routledge.

Johnson, D. 1990: *Parental Choice in Education.* London: Unwin Hyman.

MacBeath, J. and Weir, D. 1991: *Attitudes to School.* Glasgow: Jordanhill College.

McGlynn, A. and MacBeath, J. 1992: Parents and school effectiveness. Paper presented at the Centre for Educational Development, Appraisal and Research Conference, Warwick.

Merttens, R. and Vass, J. 1990: *Sharing Maths Cultures.* Basingstoke: Falmer.

Miliband, D. 1991: *Markets, Politics and Education.* London: Institute for Public Policy Research.

Mortimore, P., Sammons, P., Stoll, L., Lewis, D. and Ecob, R. 1988: *School Matters.* Wells: Open Books.

Morton, R. 1991: West Heath Junior School. In P. Mortimore and J. Mortimore (eds) *The Primary Head: Roles, Responsibilities and Reflections*, London: Paul Chapman, 32–51.

Munn, P. 1985: Accountability and parent–teacher communication. *British Educational Research Journal*, 11, 105–10.

National Union of Teachers 1991: *Evaluation of 1991 Key Stage One SATs.* London: NUT.

National Union of Teachers 1992: *Testing and Assessing 6 and 7 Year Olds.* London: NUT.

Petch, A. 1986: Parental choice at entry to primary school. *Research Papers in Education*, 1, 26–47.

Public Attitude Surveys 1989: *Parental Awareness of School Education.* High Wycombe: PAS.

Ramsay, P., Harold, B., Hawk, K., Kaai, T., Marriott, R. and Poskitt, J. 1990: *There's No Going Back: Collaborative Decision-making in Education.* Hamilton, New Zealand: University of Waikato Press.

Sexton, S. 1987: *Our Schools – A Radical Policy.* London: IEA Education Unit.

Tizard, B. and Hughes, M. 1984: *Young Children Learning.* London: Fontana.

Tizard, B., Blatchford, P., Burke, J., Farquhar, C. and Plewis, I. 1988: *Young Children at School in the Inner City.* Hove: Lawrence Erlbaum.

Tizard, J., Schofield, W.N. and Hewison, J. 1982: Collaboration between teachers and parents in assisting children's reading. *British Journal of Educational Psychology*, 52, 1–15.

Toomey, D. 1993: Can parental involvement in schools increase educational inequality? In R. Merttens, D. Mayers, A. Brown and J. Vass (eds) *Ruling the Margins: Problematising Parental Involvement*, London: University of North London Press, 131–7.

Tough, J. 1976: *Listening to Children Talking*. London: Ward Lock.

Warnock, M. 1985: Teacher teach thyself. *The Listener*, 28 March.

Wells, C.G. 1984: *Language Development in the Preschool Years*. Cambridge: Cambridge University Press.

Wells, C.G. 1987: *The Meaning Makers*. London: Hodder and Stoughton.

West, A., Davies, J. and Scott, G. 1992: Attitudes to secondary school: parents' views over a five-year period. *Research Papers in Education*, 7, 129–49.

Widlake, P. and Macleod, F. 1985: *Raising Standards*. Coventry: CEDC.

Wikeley, F. 1986: Communication between parents and teachers. *Perspectives*, 24, 38–43.

Wikeley, F. 1989: Communication between parents and teachers and their perceptions of each other. Unpublished M.Phil. thesis, University of Exeter.

Woods, P. 1993: Parents as consumer-citizens. In R. Merttens, D. Mayers, A. Brown and J. Vass (eds) *Ruling the Margins: Problematising Parental Involvement*, London: University of North London Press, 9–24.

Index

academic criteria 95–6
  see also league tables
academic standards 95–6, 97–8,
    119–21
accountability in education 7
'alternative league tables' 174
assessment 157, 172–3, 219
  see also SATs, standardised
    assessment, league tables;
    and under parents' attitudes,
    parents' knowledge
Attainment Targets 124
Audience Selection 98

Baker, K. 9–10, 13, 97
Bash, L. 10–11
Battle, S. 21
Becher, T. 148
Belfield Reading Project 6
Bennett, S.N. 175
Bernstein, B. 3
Black, P. 174
Blatch, Baroness 98
Blatchford, P. 98, 209
Boyson, R. 8
Brown, P. 12–13
Bullock Report 3
Burke, J. 98, 209

Carré, C.G. 175
Carter, D.S.G. 175

children as consumers 24, 39, 72
children's happiness as a factor
    viii, 29–30, 31, 34, 38, 39, 79,
    83–4, 90, 94, 100, 101–2, 113,
    114, 118
choice of school see under parents'
    reasons for choice of school
Clarke, K. 149
Clift, P.S. 21
Coleman, P. 209
Collinge, J. 209
Community Education
    Development Centre
    project 6
comparing schools see league
    tables
competition between schools 10,
    21, 23, 56, 78
  see also parental choice, league
    tables
comprehensive education 8
consulting parents 213–16, 217–19
'consumer-citizen' 56–7, 76
consumerism in education 56–7,
    204–5, 217
  see also competition between
    schools, parental choice
Corrigan, P. 79
Coulby, D. 10–11
Cox, C.B. 8
Cyster, R. 21

Daily Mail 175
David, M.E. 79
Davies, J. 98, 209
Dearing, Sir R. 217
Department of Education and
    Science 11, 97–8, 124–5, 149,
    172–3, 187
Desforges, C. 174, 209
Docking, J.W. 2, 5–6
Douglas, J.W.B. 3

Ecob, R. 98, 209
Education Acts 1980 and 1986 7
educational diversity 12–13
educational reform 1, 7–19, 78,
    113, 124, 203–7, 216–19
  difficulties for schools 22,
    110–11
  public attitudes to 14–15
  in Scotland 14, 175
Education Reform Act 1988 7, 9,
    10, 78, 124
Education White Paper 1992 12,
    14, 78
Edwards, A. 78, 79
Eraut, M. 148

Farquhar, C. 98, 209
findings 204–7
  generalizability of 207–10
  implications for policy 216–19
  implications for schools 210–16
Flew A. 8

Golby, M. 7
Gooch, M. 5
Graham, D. 15
grant-maintained schools 12
Griffiths, A. 6
Guardian, The 5

Hadow Report 2
Hamilton, D. 6
Hannon, P. 6
happiness *see* children's happiness as
    a factor

Haringey Reading Project 6
Harold, B. 209
Hawk, K. 209
headteachers
  effect of interviews on 52–3
  effect of reforms on 22, 34, 36
  selected for study 21–2
headteachers' attitudes / views
    regarding
  children 24
  consumerism 23–4, 25, 39, 57
  influence of media 33, 38, 40,
    99
  parental choice 26–9
  parents 20–40: as consumers
    22–6, 39, 57; as partners
    24–5, 39, 57
  parents' attitudes to reforms
    37–9, 125
  parents' criteria for good school
    29–31
  parents' informedness re reforms
    33–7, 149
  parents' lack of interest 28,
    34–5, 38, 40, 42, 149
  parents' power 28
  parents' satisfaction with
    school 31–3, 98–9
Hewison, J. 6
Hillgate Group 8, 9, 10
Holden, C. 209, 215
Hughes, M. ix, 4, 209

IMPACT project 6
Independent, The 175

Jackson, A. 6
Johnson, D. 79

Kaai, T. 209
Key Stage One 16, 153, 175
Key Stage Two 158
Knight, J. 148

Lane, B. 7
language deficit theory 3–4

league tables   11, 15, 93–6, 174, 201
Lewis, D.   98, 209
lobby of MPs   15
local management of schools   7

MacBeath, I.   148
MacGregor, J.   172–3
Macleod, F.   6
market forces *see* competition
     between schools
Marriott, R.   209
media
   influencing parents   33, 38, 40
   reporting falling standards etc.
      119, 120, 121, 123, 210, 218
   reporting on SATs   175, 176–7,
      179, 181, 184
   source of information   70, 150,
      152, 179
Merttens, R.   6
methodology   21–2, 41–3, 49–51,
      58
   analysis of data   53–4
   characteristics of sample   16,
      41–9, 54
Miliband, D.   79
Morrissey, M.   15
Mortimore, P.   98, 209
Morton, R.   215
Munn, P.   148

National Curriculum   9, 10–11,
      124–47, 148–9, 170, 172–3,
      218
   informing parents about   124–5,
      150–6
   see also under parents' attitudes,
      parents' knowledge
National Union of Teachers
      174–5, 176–7

PACT project   6
parental choice   8–13, 16–17,
      78–81, 91, 96, 204, 217–18
   arguments against   79
   complexities of issue of   80–1

effects on schools of   26–9
   at secondary level   66–8, 94
   in the United States   78
   see also parents' reasons for
      choice of school
parental roles
   see parents as consumers, parents
      as partners
   importance of   203
   tension between   7–8
parent governors   7
'parentocracy'   12–13
parents
   changing schools   43–5, 116–19
   as consumers   1–2, 7–13, 16,
      56–77, 113, 204, 207
   dropping from study   43–5
   effect of interviews on   51–3
   'know best'   12
   as partners   5–8, 211
   perceiving selves as consumers
      57–73
   as problems   2–5, 207
   visiting schools   68, 91–3
   wanting more information
      150–1, 154–5, 157, 201
parents' attitudes/views regarding
   assessment   18, 172–202, 206–7:
      see also SATs
   changing schools   112–15,
      199–200
   children's progress   111–12,
      190–4
   consumerism in education
      58–77
   core curriculum   133–42, 147,
      206: English   136–9; maths
      139–40; science   140–2
   educational reform   13–15
   foreign languages   134, 159, 166
   foundation subjects   142–6
   league tables   15, 93–6, 198–200
   National Curriculum   17, 60,
      61, 124–47, 148, 206, 218:
      negative   130–2; positive
      127–9, 131, 132

SATs 183–6, 189–202
school staff/teachers 101,
    107–11, 185–6, 210–11
standards of education 119–21,
    122–3, 218
written reports 200–1
see also parents' satisfaction with
    school
Parent's Charter 11–12, 24, 187,
    200, 211
parents' contact with school 161–70
diary findings 165–70
see also parents' involvement in
    school
parents' criteria for 'good school'
    99–104, 122
parents' degree of choice exercised
    84–91
parents' evenings 162–3
parents' individual differences
    209–10
parents' involvement in school
    5–8, 68, 69, 75, 92
parents' knowledge about
    assessment 156–8, 177–81, 206
    core curriculum 153–6
    Key Stages 153–6, 158–61
    National Curriculum 136,
        150–61, 206
    school 17–18, 136, 148–71, 206,
        218
parents' lack of choice 27, 84–7,
    91, 96, 116, 118
at secondary level 94
parents' power/powerlessness 13,
    28, 71, 76, 203
parents' reasons for changing
    schools 113, 116–19, 122
parents' reasons for choice of
    school 82–4, 87–90, 92, 93, 95
at secondary level 94–5
parents' satisfaction
    with child's progress 111–12,
        114, 115, 116, 117, 118
    with school 17, 97–123, 205,
        210–11

parents' views changing over time
    62–73, 104, 126–7, 195,
    196–7, 199, 201–2, 206–7,
    209–10
Patten, J. 14, 15, 175
Petch, A. 79–80
Plewis, I. 98, 209
Plowden Report 3
Poskitt, J. 209
private education 8, 45, 60, 65–6,
    70, 81, 116
Public Attitude Surveys 14–15,
    98, 209
public opinion polls 98, 175

Ramsay, P. 209
return to basics *see* traditional
    methods

Sammons, P. 98, 209
SATs 51, 174, 176–86, 189–202,
    207
    children's awareness of 179–81
    children's performance in
        190–3, 207
    children's reactions to 181–3,
        186
    communicating results of
        186–9, 219
    informing children about 178
    informing parents about 177–8,
        181
    parents' awareness of 177, 181
    parents' views 183–6, 189–202
    publishing results of 15, 198
    teachers' views 174–5, 176
Schofield, W.N. 6
school (written) reports 186–90
schools selected for study 21, 42
school-visiting 68, 91–3
Scott, G. 98, 209
Sexton, S. 8–9
sources of information for parents
    children 148, 152, 154, 179,
        206
    government 124–5

media   70, 150
school   33–7, 70, 161–71, 178, 206
standardized assessment   9, 10, 11,
    18, 172, 173, 174, 201, 207
    see also SATs
state education system   8
Stoll, L.   98, 209
Sunday Mirror   98

Tabin, Y.   209
teacher assessment   157, 175
Times Educational Supplement   14
Tizard, B.   ix, 4, 98, 209
Tizard, J.   6
Toomey, D.   209

Tough, J.   3
traditional methods   30–1, 42,
    135–6, 137, 147, 206
transport as a factor   27, 86, 94

Vass, J.   6

Warnock, M.   4–5
Weir, D.   148
West, A.   98, 209
Whitty, G.   78, 79
Widlake, P.   6
Wikeley, F.   ix
Woods, P.   56–7, 76, 217
Wragg, E.C.   175

KING ALFRED'S COLLEGE
LIBRARY

KING ALFRED'S COLLEGE
LIBRARY